THE GOD WHO DRAWS NEAR

'Perhaps no other writer today has read as widely in both Christian history and Christian spirituality than Michael Haykin. The fruit of his study is evident in this book, for he not only feeds us a satisfying banquet of biblical teaching on Christian spirituality, he also garnishes it with savory stories and quotations from Christian history. You'll not find Dr Haykin reinventing spirituality for the twenty-first century, but reconnecting us with the Scriptures and with wisdom of those who have walked with God before us and can give us wise counsel for walking with our timeless God in our own generation.'
DONALD S. WHITNEY *Associate Professor of Biblical Spirituality and Senior Associate Dean at The Southern Baptist Theological Seminary, Louisville, KY, and author of* Spiritual disciplines of the Christian life *and* Spiritual disciplines within the church

'Biblical and reformed spirituality was never more needed than in these post-modern times and Michael Haykin's exposition of it in these pages is both timely and judicious. With the skill of John Owen, his treatment is intentionally trinitarian: God glorifying, Christ-centred and Spirit focused. With the added skill of a first-rate historian, Haykin mines the pages of history bringing breathtaking illustrative material to help us understand the biblical parameters of godliness. A timely book; but readers should beware: reading these pages may cost you dearly, for it will require that you part with your dearest sins and in order that you may discover in Christ fullness, contentment and joy.'
DEREK W. H. THOMAS *John E. Richards Professor of Systematic and Practical Theology, RTS, Minister of Teaching, First Presbyterian Church, Jackson, MS, and Editorial Director, reformation21.org*

'In this great little book, Michael Haykin introduces the reader to the central elements of a properly biblical spirituality. Of special note are his attention to the necessity of understanding trinitarian dimensions of the Christian life and to the value of drawing on the great classics of spirituality of the past in order to live for Christ in the contemporary world. A delightful book to read and to give to friends.'
CARL R. TRUEMAN *Professor of Historical Theology and Church History at Westminster Theological Seminary Philadelphia, PA*

'So many books on "spirituality" on the shelves of Christian and secular bookstores represent little more than new age labyrinth-walking or pseudo-spiritual pandering. Michael Haykin, one of the pre-eminent evangelical scholars in this and several other areas, brings a fresh, ancient approach to biblical spirituality. He restores to spirituality the Holy Spirit, and points us to Jesus Christ. Those who long for a closer walk with Jesus — and that should be all of us — will love this book.'
RUSSELL D. MOORE *Dean of the School of Theology and Senior Vice President for Academic Administration at The Southern Baptist Theological Seminary, Louisville, KY*

'A biblical, full-orbed view of true spirituality, founded in the Word and the Spirit, in contrast to the false spirituality that deludes so many today.'
ROBERT STRIVENS *Principal-Designate, London Theological Seminary, London, UK*

THE
GOD
WHO
DRAWS
NEAR

**AN INTRODUCTION TO
BIBLICAL SPIRITUALITY**

MICHAEL A. G. HAYKIN

 EVANGELICAL PRESS

Evangelical Press
Faverdale North, Darlington, DL3 0PH England
Evangelical Press USA
P. O. Box 825, Webster, NY 14580 USA
email: sales@evangelicalpress.org
www.evangelicalpress.org

First published 2007

Unless otherwise indicated, all Scripture quotations are from *The Holy Bible: English Standard Version*, published by HarperCollins Publishers © 2001 by Crossway Bibles, a division of Good News Publishers. Used by permission. All rights reserved.

British Library Cataloguing in Publication Data available
ISBN-13 978 0 85234 638 9   ISBN 0 85234 638 7

PRINTED AND BOUND IN THE U.S.A.

*To Eric and Isabel Lindsay
and David and Ruth Kay,
for the joy and strength of their
Christian friendship*

For what great nation is there
that has a god so near to it as
the LORD our God is to us,
whenever we call upon him?
— *Deuteronomy 4:*7

We draw near to God by means.
— *Richard Greenham (1540-1594)*

CONTENTS

FOREWORD

Spirituality seems to be all the rage today. Scores of books, articles, websites, courses, and personal and group retreats are promoting spiritual formation. With its prevailing secularism and materialism, modern culture has failed to satisfy its consumers. Many are coming to realize the truth of what Moses said to the children of Israel, 'Man doth not live by bread only' (Deut. 8:3, KJV). With Christ in his Sermon on the Mount, they ask, 'Is not the life more than meat, and the body than raiment?' (Matt. 6:25, KJV). The result is a new interest in discovering and nurturing the inward, spiritual dimensions of human life.

The cultivation of spiritual life has been addressed in different ways by different Christian traditions. Roman Catholicism has offered a spirituality of ritualism and sacramental administration, and alternatively, the disciplines of monastic life and the pursuits of mysticism. The Wesleyan Methodist tradition, the Holiness movement, and more recently, Pentecostalism and the charismatic movement have offered a spirituality with less ceremonial or intellectual content and a great deal more emotion and subjectivism.

The problem with most spirituality today is that it is not closely moored in Scripture and too often degenerates into unbiblical mysticism. In contrast, Reformed Christianity has followed a path of its own, largely determined by its concern to test all things by Scripture and to develop a spiritual life shaped by Scripture's teachings and directives. *The God who draws near* shows us that Reformed spirituality is the outworking of the conviction that 'all Scripture is given by inspiration of God, and is profitable for doctrine, for reproof, for correction, for instruction in righteousness' (2 Tim. 3:16, KJV). In dependence upon the Holy Spirit, it aims to achieve what John Murray (1898-1975) called 'intelligent piety', wedding scriptural knowledge and heartfelt piety.

The dual emphasis of nurturing both the mind and the soul is sorely needed today. On the one hand, we confront the problem of dry, Reformed orthodoxy, which has correct doctrinal teaching but lacks emphasis on vibrant, godly living. The result is that people bow before the doctrine of God without a vital, spiritual union with the God of doctrine. On the other hand, Pentecostal and charismatic Christianity offers emotionalism in protest against a formal, lifeless Christianity, but it is not rooted solidly in Scripture. The result is that people bow before human feeling rather than before the triune God.

This book promotes biblical spirituality at its best, deeply rooted in God's amazing grace and the means of grace and buttressed by the Reformed and Puritan heritage. It illustrates well the testimony of D. Martyn Lloyd-Jones (1899-1981) that 'the ultimate test of our spirituality is the measure of our amazement at the grace of God'. It shows us that pursuing biblical spirituality is rooted in our need. Spirituality is not a mark of exceptional piety for which we merit anything but is a humble, grateful response to God for who he is in relation to who we are and what we know by virtue of our union with Christ. In summary, spirituality is not about a list or about mastering techniques but about the hard, slow work of becoming increasingly conformed to Jesus by the Spirit.

Dr Haykin shows us that spiritual formation is inseparable from the spiritual disciplines. We need to carry out, on a regular basis, those spiritual exercises or patterns of living that help us establish habits that lead to godliness. Let us take his well-defined, core elements of spirituality — knowledge of God, self-knowledge, Christ- and cross-centredness, the Scriptures, prayer, meditation, spiritual friendship, and missions — and seek the Spirit's grace, within these parameters, to let our lives show them to the world. As James I. Packer said, 'The way to be truly happy is to be truly human, and the way to be truly human is to be truly godly.' The calling and challenge is now ours.

JOEL R. BEEKE
President and Professor of Systematic Theology and Homiletics at Puritan Reformed Theological Seminary, Grand Rapids, MI, USA

ACKNOWLEDGEMENTS

No book is written in a vacuum. This one is no exception. It was students of Central Baptist Seminary, Toronto, whom I had the distinct privilege and pleasure of teaching from 1982 to 1993, who first heard some of what is contained in the various chapters of this book. It was in those years that I began to take an interest in the history of Christian spirituality during the Reformation, the Puritan era and eighteenth-century evangelicalism. Inevitably this interest in Protestant and evangelical spirituality found its way into lectures and chapel talks and, in the years that followed, even sermons. A number of those students were an enormous help to me as they sharpened my thinking and, I hope, helped me in my walk with God.

I am also deeply thankful for two couples who have become good friends over the past years and who have played important roles in the genesis of this book: Eric and Isabel Lindsay of Belfast, Northern Ireland, and David and Ruth Kay of Barnstaple, Devon,

England. It is with thanks to the triune God for their friendship that I dedicate this book to them.

Also before we begin, another debt needs to be acknowledged. It was reading Richard Lovelace's masterful *Dynamics of Spiritual Life: An Evangelical Theology of Renewal* (InterVarsity Press, 1979) in the early 1980s that helped me begin to understand the necessity for and contours of an evangelical spirituality. His perspective on the preconditions, primary and secondary elements of renewal and spirituality and the way in which a biblical understanding of revival needs to take into consideration the history of the church has stayed with me over the years and profoundly shaped my own thinking, writing and teaching about evangelical spirituality.[1]

INTRODUCTION

During Easter 1985, Thomas Howard — a graduate of Wheaton College and a professor of English at Gordon College, both long-standing bastions of evangelicalism, and himself the product of a staunch evangelical family, whose sister is Elisabeth Elliot, author and widow of the evangelical martyr Jim Elliot (1927-1956) — became a Roman Catholic.

Howard's conversion to Roman Catholicism caused quite a stir at the time in evangelical circles and *Christianity Today*, that quint-essential evangelical publication, ran a nine-page special report on the event. It makes for fascinating reading. When asked why he had decided to make the journey to Rome, he cited what he called the shallowness of evangelicalism. Two things in particular were mentioned. First, there was what Howard called 'the desperate, barren, parched nature of evangelical worship'. Second, there was what he described as evangelicalism's 'poverty when it comes to the deeper riches of Christian spirituality'.[1]

Howard's observation that contemporary evangelical spirituality is poor and shallow is something that many others have also apparently recognized, for a growing number of evangelicals in the past twenty-five years or so have begun to pay more attention to this vital subject. In fact, among evangelicals, 'spirituality' has become what American evangelical historian Richard Lovelace has called 'a growth industry'.[2]

At the same time, in western culture in general, there has been a marked increase of interest in 'spirituality'. Being 'spiritual' and spirituality are in vogue. In another article in *Christianity Today* (2 April 2001), Edith M. Humphrey, an evangelical scholar, commented on this upsurge of interest in our culture in spirituality. She did a random search of the web via a search engine (Metacrawler) and found the following websites devoted to this or that form of spirituality:

Spirituality for Today; Women's Spirituality Book List; The Spirited Walker: Fitness Walking for Clarity, Balance, and Spiritual Connection; ...Jesuit Spirituality; Native American Spirituality; ...Spirit Tools for a New Age (pyramids, wands, daggers, and pendulums...); Spirituality and Health; Spirituality and Living Longer; The Inner Self Magazine: Spirituality as Opposed to Religion; Spirituality in the Workplace; Sex and Spirituality: Frequently Asked Questions; Apply Spiritual Ideas in Practical Ways; Spirituality Book — the invisible Path to Success; Psychotherapy and Spirituality; The Spiritual Walk of the Labyrinth...[3]

Looking at this mish-mash, it would not be surprising if some Christians were extremely hesitant to use the term 'spirituality'. The word seems to mean everything — and consequently mean nothing.

And yet the word 'spirituality' can and should be used in a Christian context, for it reminds us of something very basic about the Christian life. The word 'spirituality' comes from a Latin term, *spiritualitas*, which, in turn, is derived from the word *spiritus*, the Latin word for 'spirit'. The earliest recorded use of *spiritualitas* is in the fifth century, when an anonymous writer, possibly Faustus of Riez (died *c.* A.D. 490), tells a correspondent to 'so act as to advance in spirituality (*in spiritualitate*)'.[4] From the surrounding context, it is clear that the author is urging his correspondent to live a life in accord with the Holy Spirit. This is an excellent doorway into the understanding of this term. True spirituality is intimately bound up with the Holy Spirit and his work.

SPIRITUALITY TIED TO THE HOLY SPIRIT'S WORK

If we ask the New Testament authors, 'What is the nature of the Spirit's work?', we receive a plethora of information. It is the Holy Spirit, for example, who is the one who makes God's love real for us — 'God's love has been poured into our hearts through the Holy Spirit' (Rom. 5:5). In a sense, it is he who stands at the threshold of the Christian life, for only he can enable us to embrace Christ as Saviour and Lord — 'no one can say "Jesus is Lord" except in the Holy Spirit' (1 Cor. 12:3). Then, it is the Spirit who gives us the boldness to come into the presence of the awesome and almighty Maker of heaven and earth and call him 'Dear Father' — 'God has sent the Spirit of his Son into our hearts, crying, "Abba! Father!"' (Gal. 4:6). It is the Spirit who enables believers, from various racial, social and religious backgrounds, to find true unity in Christ and together worship God (Eph. 2:18). In fact, without the Spirit, worship and the glorification of Jesus Christ cannot take place (Phil. 3:3). And it is the Spirit who is the true Guarantor of orthodoxy (2 Tim. 1:14).

An excellent summary statement of the range of the Spirit's work is Galatians 5:25, which speaks so plainly about the Spirit as the Source from which we are to live our lives: 'If we live by the Spirit, let us also walk by the Spirit.' The Spirit thus undergirds and empowers the entirety of our lives as Christians. To paraphrase John 15:5: apart from the Holy Spirit, we can do nothing of any true eternal value. The English Nathanael Ranew (*c.*1602-1678)[5] has rightly summarized the Spirit's new-covenant ministry in the following way:

> The Holy Spirit first comes to the soul and person of a Christian, applies Christ to him, brings Christ into him, makes him his temple, and a habitation of God and Christ to dwell in the heart. The Spirit comes, inhabits, sweeps, and cleanses; furnishes the heart with light, that was darkness; with truth, that was error and deceitfulness; with power, that was weakness; life, warmth and qualifications of heavenly graces, that was cold, dead, and altogether sinful; and draws the glorious image of Christ upon the soul. He enlivens, establishes, enlarges, and encourages, and fills the spirit with peace and joy unspeakable.[6]

In this introduction to biblical spirituality, we will look at nine marks of the Spirit's work as he makes real God's drawing near to us.[7] This sort of reflection on the Spirit's work is nothing new. The Puritans and early evangelicals excelled in it. One thinks, for instance, of *The Religious Affections* (1746) by Jonathan Edwards (1703-1758), which is far more than simply a response to the fanaticism that appeared during the Great Awakening in America. It is part of a long history of serious reflection on what true piety looks like. In a sense, then, this small book is part of this larger tradition of spiritual reflection.

*'The undivided three
and the mysterious One'*

CHAPTER ONE

A trinitarian
SPIRITUALITY

Matthew 28:19-20 has long been described as the Great Commission, that is, the responsibility of the church to take the gospel cross-culturally to other nations around the world. William Carey (1761-1834), for example, employed it to awaken his fellow Calvinistic Baptists to this great biblical truth. Some theologians had argued that the command to make disciples from all the nations was no longer incumbent upon the church. The early church, they maintained, had actually *fulfilled* that command. Moreover, according to Carey, they argued that:

> …we have enough to do to attend to the salvation of our own countrymen; and that, if God intends the salvation of the heathen, he will some way or other bring them to the gospel, or the gospel to them.[1]

Carey ably refuted this entire argument by pointing out that two other aspects of this Matthean text had no temporal limitations on them. The command to baptize was still very much in force and the promise of Christ's abiding presence was still a comfort in time of trouble and turmoil. 'Pity therefore', Carey concluded, 'humanity, and much more Christianity, call loudly for every possible exertion to introduce the gospel' amongst the unbelieving nations of the world.[2]

This is certainly a vital insight into this text. But there is one more basic. We need to listen afresh to what this text tells us about knowing God. In a word, this text tells us that to truly know God is to know him as a triune Being — Father, Son and Holy Spirit. We will see how this insight is part and parcel of the entire New Testament revelation about God. We also will explore the profound implications that this fact, which the church has called the doctrine of trinity, has for evangelical spirituality.

PAUL: A TRINITARIAN THEOLOGIAN

Let us look more closely at the New Testament evidence for the trinity. There are numerous passages in the Pauline *corpus*, for example, where the Father, the Son and the Holy Spirit are linked together as co-Sources of the blessings that belong to Christians. There is the way in which Paul, in 1 Corinthians 12:4-6, traces the various manifestations of God's grace in the church first to the Spirit, then to the Lord Jesus and finally to God: 'There are diversities of gifts, but the same Spirit. There are differences of ministries, but the same Lord. And there are diversities of activities, but it is the same God who works all in all.' One should not regard the three phrases 'diversities of gifts', 'differences of ministries' and 'diversities of activities' as three separate items. Rather, these are three different ways of looking at the same thing: the gifts of the Spirit as they manifest themselves in the life of a Christian community. Paul's interest here is clearly demonstrating that the diversity of gifts in the church is traceable back to one and the same God. He is not seeking to argue for the reality of the trinity. Yet, he surely assumes that the Spirit, the

Lord Jesus Christ and the Father are One. [3]

We see the same assumption at work in Ephesians 4:4-6, where Paul outlines the trinitarian basis of walking worthily of the Christian calling. After giving the exhortation to his readers in Ephesians 4:1 to 'walk in a manner worthy of the calling to which you have been called', the apostle spells out what this entails in verses 2-3, and then in verses 4-6 he gives the basis for this exhortation. 'There is one body and one Spirit', he writes, 'just as you were called to the one hope that belongs to your call — one Lord, one faith, one baptism, one God and Father of all, who is over all, and through all, and in all.' Again notice how Paul is not seeking to develop a doctrine of the trinity — how Spirit, Son and Father are one God. Yet, it is clear that both his and his readers' experience of God in the Christian life can be adequately expressed only in trinitarian terms.[4]

In Titus 3:4-6 we have yet another trinitarian passage. In verse 3 Paul begins with a particularly vivid description of the way both he and his hearers once were: 'foolish, disobedient, led astray, slaves to various passions and pleasures, passing our days in malice and envy, hated by others and hating one another'. Totally unable to extricate themselves from this state, it was God alone who enabled them to break free. Thus we read in verses 4-6: 'When the goodness and loving kindness of God our Saviour appeared, he saved us, not because of works done by us in righteousness, but according to his own mercy, by the washing of regeneration and renewal of the Holy Spirit, whom he poured out on us richly through Jesus Christ our Saviour.'

There are certainly phrases in this passage that are not the easiest to understand. The phrase 'the washing of regeneration and renewal of the Holy Spirit', for example, has been the subject of much debate, though it is probably best understood as that inner cleansing which the Holy Spirit effects when he regenerates and renews the mind and heart of the new convert.[5] What is clear, though, is that it is God who saves men and women from bondage to sin and hate. But notice that Christ is also described as our

'Saviour', the identical term that is given to God the Father. God saves sinners but not, and never, apart from Christ. To describe Christ as Saviour is surely an implicit confession of his deity. But the Spirit also must be divine, for it is through his being poured out upon sinners that they are actually converted. If Christ and the Spirit are anything less than God, then the affirmation at the beginning of the passage, that it is God who saves, makes no sense.

Or think about the benediction in 2 Corinthians 13:14: 'The grace of the Lord Jesus Christ and the love of God and the fellowship of the Holy Spirit be with you all.' New Testament scholar Gordon Fee believes that this 'benediction is the most profound theological moment in the Pauline corpus'.[6] It captures, on the one hand, the heart of Paul's doctrine of salvation: God's loving determination to save his people through the Lord Jesus Christ's suffering and death, the supreme and concrete manifestation of God's grace and the ongoing appropriation of that grace through the Holy Spirit. On the other hand, Fee notes that 2 Corinthians 13:14 serves as a passageway into Paul's understanding of God. The grace of God that lies at the base of the Christian life is found only in Christ and through the Spirit. For Paul, to truly encounter God in a meaningful way is to deal with Jesus Christ and the Holy Spirit. Fee puts it well when he states for Paul 'to be Christian one must finally understand God in a trinitarian way'.[7]

FURTHER NEW TESTAMENT WITNESS

In other parts of the New Testament the same truths are to be observed. Even outside of Paul's letters 'it is everywhere assumed that the redemptive activities of God rest on a threefold source in God the Father, the Lord Jesus Christ and the Holy Spirit'.[8] Consider the following evidence.

- 1 Peter 1:2: Here, in his first letter, Peter can speak of God's saints in various regions of Asia Minor as being chosen 'according to the foreknowledge of God the Father, in the sanctification of the Spirit, for obedience to Jesus Christ and for sprinkling with his blood'.

• Jude 20-21: Jude writes his brief letter to encourage his readers to stand firm against apostasy by first of all praying in the Holy Spirit, then keeping themselves in the love of God and finally waiting for the mercy of the Lord Jesus Christ.

• Revelation 1:4-5: the author asks for the seven churches to whom he writes 'grace…and peace' from a three-fold Source: first, 'from him who is and who was and who is to come', a reference to God the Father that is based on Exodus 3:14; then, from 'the seven Spirits who are before his throne', which is probably to be understood as a figurative reference to the Holy Spirit;[9] and finally, 'from Jesus Christ'.

Particularly rich in trinitarian language is the Gospel of John.[10] In his farewell discourse (John 14 – 16), Jesus tells his disciples 'the Holy Spirit, whom the Father will send in my name, he will teach you all things, and bring to your remembrance all that I have said to you' (John 14:26). Other verses in this section of John's Gospel, however, assert that Jesus will be the One who will send the Spirit (John 15:26; 16:7). The Spirit is being sent in the place of Jesus as '*another* Helper' or Advocate (John 14:16). It is only through the Spirit's presence in the disciples' lives that Jesus and the Father are also present (John 14:23).

Like the other New Testament authors John does not use the word 'trinity' — that word was not coined until the late second century when the North African theologian Tertullian (fl. A.D.190-215) came up with it — but all of the key elements of trinitarian faith are already here.[11]

MATTHEW 28:19: AFFIRMING THE TRINITY

With this survey of some of the trinitarian texts of the New Testament as a backdrop we can return to the baptismal formula of Matthew 28:19: 'Go therefore and make disciples of all nations, baptizing them in the name of the Father and of the Son and of the Holy Spirit.' As Benjamin B. Warfield (1851-1921) has noted, this text is 'the nearest approach to a formal announcement of the doctrine of the Trinity which is recorded from Our Lord's lips'.[12] Three observations regarding what this verse has to teach us about God can be made.

First, we find the names of the Father, the Son and the Holy Spirit coordinated in such a way as to imply their equality. The little conjunction 'and' (*kai*) that artlessly links them together indicates that here we are dealing with three co-equal, and therefore divine, subjects. This is reinforced by the observation made by that great fourth-century defender of the doctrine of the trinity, Athanasius of Alexandria (*c.* A.D. 299-373), during the Arian controversy that it would be very odd for baptism to be into the name of 'God and a creature'.[13]

Second, it is noteworthy that the baptismal formula does not say 'in the name of the Father, Son and Holy Spirit'. There is a definite article used before each of the three: 'in the name of *the* Father and *the* Son and *the* Holy Spirit'. The former might be taken to mean that the three are simply designations of one and the same person. But that is the heresy of Modalism, which essentially suggests that the different members of the Godhead are actually masks put on successively by one and the same person during various stages of divine activity.[14] No, the use of the definite article on each occasion helps safeguard the fact that the Father, the Son and the Holy Spirit are indeed three distinct persons.

Nor does the baptismal formula run this way: 'in the names of the Father and the Son and the Holy Spirit'. Mention is made only of the singular *name* of the three, which is a distinct indication of their unity.[15] In other words, neither this passage nor the other New Testament texts we have looked at already compromise the monotheism that the apostolic church had inherited from the Old Testament. Christianity does not believe in three separate gods! There is one God. Thus, we are baptized into 'the name' — singular — 'of the Father and of the Son and of the Holy Spirit'.

THE TRINITY AND CHRISTIAN SPIRITUALITY

But what are the implications of all this for Christian spirituality?

The first implication for Christian spirituality is to remain balanced in the way we think about God. In the past some evangelicals have had a tendency to focus on Christ to the exclusion of the other persons of the Godhead. And in this past century, certain Pentecostals and charismatics have been Spirit-oriented to a very unhealthy degree. As J. I. Packer has correctly noted: 'False proportions in our doctrine are the beginning of false doctrine itself.'[16] We are to treasure each of the divine persons and their work in our lives. Let the following testimony, that of the Welsh poetess Ann Griffiths (1776-1805), be a warning in this regard. Converted around 1797, she became one of the great hymnwriters of Welsh Calvinistic Methodism. In a letter that she wrote to a friend named Elizabeth Evans she admitted:

> Dear sister, the most outstanding thing that is on my mind at present as a matter for thought is to do with grieving the Holy Spirit. This word came into my mind, 'Know ye not that your bodies are temples of the Holy Spirit which dwelleth in you' [1 Cor. 6:19]. And on penetrating a little into the wonders of the Person, and how he dwells or resides in the believer, I think in short that I have never been possessed to the same degree by reverential fears of grieving him, and along with this I have been able to see one reason, and the chief reason, why this great sin has made such a slight impression and weighed so lightly upon my mind, on account of my base and blasphemous thoughts about a Person so great.
>
> This is how my thoughts ran about the Persons of the Trinity. I feel my mind being seized by shame, and even inhibited from speaking on account of the harmfulness of this. I thought of the Persons of the Father and the Son as co-equal; but as for the Person of the Holy Spirit, I regarded him as a functionary subordinate to them. O what a misguided imagination about a Person who is divine, all-present, all-

knowing, and all-powerful to carry on and complete the good work which he has begun in accordance with the covenant of grace and the counsel of the Three in One regarding those who are the objects of the primal love. O for the privilege of being one of their number.[17]

What is so striking about this text is the genuine depth of feeling displayed with regard to what some might consider a theological error of little consequence. But Ann is right to recognize that when it comes to the trinity, not giving each of the members of the God-head their proper due is harmful at best, blasphemous at worst.

Second, by being baptized into 'the name of the Father and the Son and the Holy Spirit' Christians are affirming their faith in that God who has revealed himself in the Scriptures as the Father and the Son and the Holy Spirit. As we have been baptized so we believe.[18] They are asserting that to know God is to know him as a triune Being.

Since the tragic events of 11 September 2001 we have heard the term 'God' voiced in public over and over again. For instance, shortly after those horrific events American talk-show host Larry King had a fascinating show entitled 'September 11: Where Was God?' He had an interesting panel of guests. From San Diego there was the New Age guru Deepak Chopra, the best-selling author of *How to Know God*. From Boston, Rabbi Harold Kushner, another best-selling author, best known for his *When Bad Things Happen to Good People*. Based in Los Angeles was Dr Maher Hathout, an Islamics scholar and senior adviser to the Muslim Public Affairs Council. And finally two evangelical Christians: from Atlanta, Bruce Wilkinson, the best-selling author of *The Prayer of Jabez* and all of its spin-offs, and the founder of the Walk Through the Bible Ministries; and from Sun Valley, California, John MacArthur, pastor of the Grace Community Church, best-selling author, and president of The Masters College and Seminary.[19]

Obviously much was said about God given the topic under discussion. But really only Wilkinson and MacArthur were able to speak about the true God, that One who has revealed himself definitively in the person and work of Jesus Christ and who makes that revelation known to human beings through his Holy Spirit. All other gods are idols, creations of men's minds and hearts. To know God is to know him as a triune Being. The twentieth-century Swiss theologian Karl Barth (1886-1968), though we have disagreements with him in other areas, was spot on when he said: 'Trinity is the Christian name for God.'[20]

But if it is the case that Christians know the true and living God, it is not the case that we know him *exhaustively*. The doctrine of the trinity well displays how much we do not know about God. What human being, no matter how learned, can fully understand how God can be One and yet three? Here is a deep mystery, the deepest of mysteries. What human mind can fathom the oneness and the threeness of God?

This mystery of mysteries is given fabulous expression in 'We give immortal praise' by Isaac Watts (1674-1748), the Congregationalist hymnwriter often described as the father of the English hymn. The first three stanzas of this hymn outline the work of each member of the Godhead in securing the salvation of sinful men and women: the Father's love which stands at the fountainhead of that salvation; the Son's death which effects redemption; and the Spirit's 'new-creating power' that applies the Son's work to sinners' hearts and so 'completes the great design'. Watts continues:

> Almighty God, to thee
>   Be endless honour done,
> The undivided Three,
>   And the mysterious One.
> Where reason fails,
>   With all her powers —
> There faith prevails,
>   And love adores.

This final stanza unashamedly confesses that God is both 'the undivided Three' and 'the mysterious One'. For Watts the mystery obviously concerns how the three can be said to be one. The essential unity of the three is something that ultimately human reason, even 'with all her powers', cannot fathom. The proper response to this mystery was not therefore to reject it as irrational, as so many were doing in the eighteenth century.[21] Although it is far above human comprehension to fathom, the doctrine of the trinity is not irrational. In the face of this mystery logic and human reason can only go so far. But, thanks be to God, faith and love can go where reason cannot.

Finally, we should note that baptism into the name of the triune God implies more than a belief in and knowledge of the trinity. It speaks of obedience and worship. To be baptized 'into the name of the Father and of the Son and of the Holy Spirit' is to enter into a 'relationship of belonging to the triune God'.[22] We have become his and living for him and worshipping him are increasingly our supreme delight. And in this way we have a foretaste of the beatific vision when we shall experience the reality of which the following words speak:

> To the great One-in-Three,
>   Eternal praises be,
>   Hence, evermore.
> His sovereign majesty
>   May we in glory see,
> And to eternity
>   Love and adore![23]

CHAPTER TWO

Knowing God
AND KNOWING OURSELVES

In 1 Timothy 1:5 we read the apostle Paul's conviction that the ultimate goal of his Christian teaching and doctrinal instruction was to develop love in his hearers — love for God and love for one's fellow human beings. Richard Lovelace makes the same point in his book *Renewal as a Way of Life: A Guidebook for Spiritual Growth*: 'the goal of authentic spirituality is a life which escapes from the closed circle of self-indulgence, or even self-improvement, to become absorbed in the love of God and other persons'.[1]

GOD AT THE CENTRE

Self-centred spirituality is the prime characteristic of pagan culture, be it ancient or modern. Again, Richard Lovelace can state: 'Self-knowledge and self-fulfillment are considered to be the core of human achievement' by pagan culture.[2] Self-knowledge is not wrong *per se*, but it must be pursued in the light of the knowledge of God.

This latter point is the famous starting-point of the *Institutes of the Christian Religion*, the *magnum opus* of John Calvin (1509–1564). In the opening pages of this work, the French Reformer maintains that true wisdom consists of two parts: knowledge of God and self-knowledge. The question is: which comes first, which is more basic? Calvin's answer is that the two are deeply and inextricably intertwined. Genuine self-examination leads to an awareness of one's deep limitations. We come to see that we are dependent upon God for all that we are and have. In Calvin's words: 'From the feeling of our own ignorance, vanity, poverty, infirmity, and — what is more — depravity and corruption, we recognize that the true light of wisdom, sound virtue, full abundance of every good, and purity of righteousness rest in the Lord alone.'

Within the borders of the universe that humanity inhabits there are two types of beings. There are those beings that are dependent on another. They encompass everything from elephants to snails, from angels and demons to galaxies and suns, from human beings to viruses. Then, there is that One Being, upon whom all of this depends. He alone is self-existent — the great Yahweh, the One who told Moses that his name was 'I AM WHO I AM' (Exod. 3:14). All other beings draw their sustenance and existence from him. He is utterly unique in that he has no need of anything outside of himself. He alone possesses what students of theology (the study of God) call aseity, the attribute of self-existence. And in giving life and being to all of creation, from the greatest object to the smallest particle, he is to be confessed as the one and only Creator.

But it is only as we come to know God that we really begin to know ourselves. In the 1560 French version of the *Institutes*, Calvin puts it this way: 'In knowing God, each of us also knows himself.' In his 1559 edition of the *Institutes* he speaks thus: 'It is certain that man never achieves a clear knowledge of himself unless he has first looked upon God's face…'[3]

As Calvin develops this most basic of issues concerning human experience and discusses the human encounter with the living

God of the Scriptures, it becomes clear that such an encounter is 'a deeply unsettling experience'.[4] Man before the majesty of God is humbled, feels himself undone and sees something of his sinful heart's core.[5] Without such a revelation of our true nature outside of Christ, there can be no true spirituality. The first step on setting out on the spiritual journey is to know ourselves as we truly are.

THE HOLINESS OF THE LORD IN ISAIAH

God's holiness and justice are common themes to both the Old and New Testaments. To quote Lovelace:

> [B]oth the Old and New Testaments strongly emphasize the justice of God, his fatherly displeasure with sin in his children, and his holy anger against the rebellion and cruelty of those who are his enemies. ...Jesus' persistent warnings of divine judgment of unrepentant sinners, not merely within time but for eternity, are echoed by all the New Testament writers — even by John, the apostle of love. Although the New Covenant accents God's grace, it retains the Old Testament emphasis on his justice.[6]

One of the classical descriptions of God's holiness in the human encounter with the living God is found in Isaiah 6:1-5:

> In the year that King Uzziah died I saw the Lord sitting upon a throne, high and lifted up; and the train of his robe filled the temple. Above him stood the seraphim. Each had six wings: with two he covered his face, and with two he covered his feet, and with two he flew. And one called to another and said: 'Holy, holy, holy is the LORD of hosts; the whole earth is full of his glory!' And the foundations of the thresholds shook at the voice of him who called, and the house was filled with smoke. And I said: 'Woe is me! For I am lost; for I am a man of unclean lips, and I dwell in the

midst of a people of unclean lips; for my eyes have seen the King, the LORD of Hosts!'

In this text God is revealed as a holy God, sovereign and omnipotent over all of his creation, especially angelic and human. The effect of the revelation of God's holiness upon fallen humanity is graphically described in the way that Isaiah — God's prophet — knows himself to be, above all, a sinner, whose mouth, polluted as it is, well expresses the pollution of his heart.

Nothing is said about how the vision came to Isaiah, for everything is focused upon the One whom he sees: 'in the year that King Uzziah died I saw the Lord'. Moreover, it is noteworthy that Isaiah makes no attempt to describe what God looked like. He simply mentions that he saw the Lord 'sitting upon a throne, high and lifted up; and the train of his robe filled the temple'. The King of Judah may be dead, but the Lord was still sitting upon his throne. This description of God as sitting upon a throne portrays him functioning as a king.

When someone in our western world hears the word 'king', any number of things might come to mind. Fairy tales, possibly; plays of William Shakespeare, in which kings and queens abound; photographs of royalty gathered for the wedding of Charles and Diana or for Diana's sad funeral. But for Isaiah and for the people of his day, the king was *the* government. The portrayal of the Lord in this manner thus emphasizes the fact that God is omnipotent, that none of his plans and purposes can fail to come to pass. The phrase that follows reinforces this portrayal of the authority of God. He is 'high and exalted' over all in this universe.

But God is not only all-powerful, he is also omnipresent. There is no place in the universe that is exempt from his glorious presence. Isaiah, unable to gaze upon God's face, looks down and finds that the skirts of God's robes fill the temple in which he is standing. But not only is the temple in Jerusalem filled with the glory of God's presence, but so is the earth. As the seraphim cry out to one another, 'the whole earth is full of his glory' (Isa. 6:3).[7]

The King of Heaven does not appear alone to the prophet, rather heavenly attendants —the seraphim — surround him, just as an earthly king is surrounded by the members of his court. These seraphim, of whom there is no mention elsewhere in the Old Testament, are clearly an order of angelic beings who minister to the Lord with unceasing praise and service. Yet even these heavenly beings dare not look upon the face of their Creator; but in reverent awe and humility they shield their faces and feet. Isaiah sees them standing above the throne of their Lord, ever ready to obey his commands. He hears them proclaiming one to another, in a mighty fugue, the holiness of their Creator: 'Holy, holy, holy is the Lord of hosts; the whole earth is full of his glory!' (Isa. 6:3). These seraphim are conscious that there is only One who is worthy of their adoration and praise, for he alone is intrinsically holy.

To call God 'holy' is first of all to speak of his transcendence over the entire created realm and to affirm his total independence from his creation, which could not exist for a second without him. In the words of Richard Lovelace: 'God's holiness is his differentness, for the word *holy* means "separate or distinct". God is different from all created beings.'[8] Then, in a derivative meaning, his holiness speaks of his moral purity, as Isaiah 6:5 goes on to imply.

The effect of this vision upon Isaiah is devastating and trau-matic: 'Woe is me! For I am lost; for I am a man of unclean lips, and I dwell in the midst of a people of unclean lips; for my eyes have seen the King, the Lord of Hosts!' It is only on the basis of a proper view of God, that man can attain a true estimation of himself. Now that Isaiah has seen the authority and majesty of the Lord, he sees himself as he really is — as all men actually are. He is a man whose sinful heart has polluted his lips and so prevented him from joining the song of the seraphim, as they praise their Lord with lips that are pure and stainless and free from sin. And if he cannot join in the praise of the seraphim, how much more are his polluted lips unfit to speak for God!

As the vision of Isaiah 6 unfolds, God reveals himself also as a God of mercy, for he goes on to cleanse the prophet with a 'burning coal' from the altar in Jerusalem (Isa. 6:6). But before we look at how God cleanses his people in the New Covenant era,[9] let us reflect further on this central truth about what it means to be human.

KNOWING THE DEPTH OF HUMAN SIN

One important set of biblical texts that deal with human sinfulness in believers are the letters of the apostle Paul. In the providence of God, one of the reasons for their being in the canon of Scripture is to provide Christian theology with clear teaching on the nature of the human condition and its consequent need of salvation.

One of the key terms that Paul uses to describe human sinfulness is the 'flesh' (*sarx*). The usage of this term varies throughout Paul's writings. In 1 Corinthians 15:39 it is used to describe either the physical flesh as distinct from the skeletal structure or possibly it is being used as a synonym for the whole body. In Romans 1:3 it is nothing less than the entirety of physical existence. Galatians 1:16 uses the word to mean 'human beings'.

But Paul normally uses the word with a profoundly negative connotation. When he uses it thus, it stands for the whole human personality — body, soul, mind, and emotions — as it functions in independent self-sufficiency, apart from God and the control of his Holy Spirit.[10] A good example of this latter usage is Galatians 5:16-18, where the apostle lists the 'works of the flesh'.

What does the 'flesh' entail when it has this more negative colouring? It is that in the human person which is utterly and irrevocably opposed to the Spirit of God. The flesh is oriented towards self. As Lovelace remarks,

The flesh is deeply *self-centered*. Ultimately it looks at all issues from a selfish perspective. 'What's in it for me?' is the question it invariably asks. It produces many ingenious compounds: self-confidence, self-consciousness, self-importance, self-indulgence, self-pity, self-righteousness, self-satisfaction, self-fulfillment. [11]

A state of war thus marks the relationship between the flesh and the Holy Spirit. It is a war in which there is no neutral ground. Look at what flesh seeks to encourage: 'sexual immorality, impurity, sensuality, idolatry, sorcery, enmity, strife, jealousy, fits of anger, rivalries, dissensions, divisions, envy, drunkenness, orgies' (Gal. 5:19-21). How radically different is the path on which Spirit is directing the believer: 'the fruit of the Spirit is love, joy, peace, patience, kindness, goodness, faithfulness, gentleness, self-control' (Gal. 5:22-23).

The result of this conflict, as deadly as any war fought on this planet, is that one cannot do what one wants to do. Unless defeated by a greater power, the sin within our human frame will keep us from doing the good we desire (Gal. 5:17). The central solution that Paul gives us is the presence and power of the Spirit. Thus, he writes, 'walk by the Spirit, and you will not gratify the desires of the flesh' (Gal. 5:16). This conflict is so intense, that unless one wholly leans on the Spirit, sin will triumph. And the Spirit, true to his Christocentric bent, points men and women to the unique sacrifice of the Son at the cross as *the* supreme place of cleansing from the pollution of sin and *the* strong resource in the face of sin's power.[12] As the Puritan divine John Owen (1616-1683) says, 'There is no death of sin without the death of Christ. …The Spirit alone brings the cross of Christ into our hearts with its sin-killing power; for by the Spirit we are baptized into the death of Christ.'[13]

A BALANCED PERSPECTIVE

In the history of the church some Christians have regarded this conflict as the result of a lack of faith or spirituality. The Wesleyan/ Holiness tradition is particularly prone to this perspective. Building upon the theological perspectives of John Wesley (1703-1791) and his lieutenant John Fletcher (1729-1785), many Christians in the nineteenth-century Holiness movement 'believed that it was possible for believers to live a perfect life without sin. They were able to believe this because they had redefined sin as conscious wilful acts of disobedience to known laws.'[14]

But the truth of the matter is quite different. Those who claim to have attained sinless perfection have simply not come to grips with the fact that the whole of our being is permeated with the poison of sin. Kenneth Prior employs an apt example to illustrate the human condition:

> Sin is like a drop of ink in a glass of water. It is diffused throughout the glass. The water may be only slightly blue, but nonetheless the entire contents of the glass are colored to some degree.[15]

Sin, as the transgression of God's law, produces in man a twofold need: freedom from the guilt of sin and cleansing from its defilement. The first need has been met through the death of Christ, by which we are justified (Rom. 5:1; 8:1-2), while the second need is satisfied by the work of sanctification. The believer has been delivered from being under the tyranny of sin and being sin's slave (Rom. 6:17-22). Yet, sin's presence has not been eradicated from the believer's life. Sin may have lost its dominion, but it can still bring shame, spiritual defeat and confusion into the life of a Christian.

Scottish theologian Sinclair Ferguson uses the imagery of addiction to describe this ongoing struggle with the flesh and sin: 'Although I have been delivered from addiction to sin, its presence remains. I experience withdrawal symptoms and remain weakened by its devastating impact on my life.'[16] And, as Ferguson further notes, rather than the empowering presence of Spirit in the believer's life bringing deliverance from this spiritual warfare, 'it is the presence of the Spirit that produces these conflicts'.[17] Sanctification is a progressive work, an ongoing process that is begun at regeneration but is never completed in this life.

Having said all this, we must remember, as Lovelace puts it:

Walking with God is essentially a positive thing. The Bible
does not point us toward constant introspection. Instead,
it helps us to focus on the privileges of being in Christ and
enjoying fellowship with God. This is the emphasis we have
already seen in Paul: 'Walk in the Spirit, and you will not
fulfill the desires of the flesh.' If we concentrate on fellowship with the Spirit and are led by him, then we will not be
overcome and carried out of God's will by natural drives.[18]

FROM THE VANTAGE-POINT OF A PURITAN

The past decades have witnessed a massive resurgence of interest
in the Puritans, and central to this resurgence have been the
works of John Owen, who, in his own lifetime, was dubbed the
'Calvin of England'.[19] J. I. Packer has rightly noted that 'Owen
is to be bracketed with such [theological giants] as Augustine,
Luther, Calvin, Edwards, Spurgeon, and Lloyd-Jones; he is one
of the all-time masters.'[20] Owen is particularly adept in laying
bare the human heart. Though our technological and historical
circumstances are very different from those of the Puritan era,
the hearts of men and women have not changed, as Owen shows
in his *The Nature, Power, Deceit, and Prevalency of the Remainders
of Indwelling Sin in Believers* (1667).[21] Basing his discussion on
Romans 7:21, Owen argues that sin is an ever-present reality with
which all believers must reckon. If they do not resist it by prayer
and meditation, slowly but surely it will eat away zeal for and
delight in the things of God.

A second searching work in this regard is Owen's *Of Temptation*,
which was first published in 1658 and consists of sermon material
preached during the 1650s.[22] Essentially an exposition of Matthew
26:4, it analyzes the way in which believers fall into sin. Central
again among the remedies that Owen recommends is prayer. His
pithy remark in this regard is typically Puritan: 'If we do not abide
in prayer, we shall abide in cursed temptations.'[23]

A third work that deals with this issue of sanctification is *The Mortification of Sin in Believers* (1656), which in some ways is the richest of the three.[24] Originally sermons that Owen preached in the University of Oxford during the mid-1650s, it is based on Romans 8:13 and lays out a strategy for fighting indwelling sin and warding off temptation. Owen emphasizes that in the fight against sin the Holy Spirit employs all of our human powers. In sanctifying us, Owen insists, the Spirit works

> in us and upon us, as we are fit to be wrought in and upon; that is, so as to preserve our own liberty and free obedience. He works upon our understandings, wills, consciences, and affections, agreeably to their own natures; he works in us and with us, not against us or without us; so that his assistance is an encouragement as to the facilitating of the work, and no occasion of neglect as to the work itself.[25]

Yet, Owen is very much aware that sanctification is also a gift. This duty, he writes, is only 'effected, carried on, and accomplished by the power of the Spirit'.[26] Not without reason does Owen then lovingly describe the Spirit in *The Nature, Power, Deceit, and Prevalency of the Remainders of Indwelling Sin in Believers* as 'the great beautifier of souls'.[27]

'The Holy Spirit always keeps
sweet company with Jesus Christ'

CHAPTER THREE

A Christ-centred

SPIRITUALITY

In the 'Introduction', a number of the activities of the Holy Spirit were mentioned — a small sampling of the many things ascribed to him by Scripture. In all of this activity is there one thing above all that the Spirit is seeking to do? Is there, in other words, a centre to his work and ministry in the lives of Christians?

'HE WILL BRING GLORY TO ME'

An answer to these questions can be readily found in John 16:13-14, verses which record important words that Jesus spoke to his disciples on the night of his betrayal:

> When the Spirit of truth comes, he will guide you into all the truth, for he will not speak on his own authority, but whatever he hears he will speak, and he will declare to you the things that are to come. He will glorify me, for he will take what is mine and declare it to you.

In the surrounding context Jesus is assuring his disciples that they will not be left alone when he returns to the Father after the cross and resurrection. Jesus will still be present with them, but not now via his incarnate presence but rather by means of his Holy Spirit. He is thus helping them understand something of the ministry of the Holy Spirit after what we call Pentecost.

Now, in the words 'He will bring glory to me', we have set forth for us what J. I. Packer calls the 'Holy Spirit's distinctive new covenant role', namely, 'directing all attention away from himself to Christ and drawing folk into the faith, hope, love, obedience, adoration, and dedication, which constitute communion with Christ'. This ministry of the Spirit in relation to Christ is what Packer goes on to call 'a floodlight ministry'.[1]

Since 1985 I have had the privilege nearly every year of teaching at Séminaire Baptiste Évangélique du Québec, in Montreal, Canada (SEMBEQ), the French Fellowship Baptist seminary in the west end of Montreal, located on Gouin Boulevard. The building that houses the seminary used to be a school and is located in a very prestigious area of the West Island of Montreal. I recall vividly one summer night after I had taught all day. I had decided to go for a walk in the neighbourhood. I noticed that a good number of the owners of the wealthy homes in the area had strategically placed floodlights around their homes so that passers-by like myself might 'ooh' and 'aah' about their achievements in stone and brick.

Now, if instead of focusing on the homes which were lit by the floodlights I had instead concentrated my attention on the floodlights themselves — 'Oh, that's an interesting-looking floodlight; I wonder where they bought it?' or 'What a lovely light that floodlight is giving; I wonder how powerful it is?' — I would have missed the whole meaning and purpose of the floodlights. The owners of the homes had put the floodlights out in front so that I should look at their homes, not at the floodlights, the source of illumination.

So it is with the Spirit's ministry. He has been sent by God the Father to focus our attention to Christ, to kindle in our hearts an unquenchable love for Christ and for his purposes, and to enable us to reflect faithfully his person and character. The Spirit has not come primarily to speak about himself. He has not been given to us so that we should focus primarily on him and his work. He has come to inhabit these mortal frames so that we should love Christ and adore him and that we should seek to live each day in obedience to Jesus. The work and ministry of the Holy Spirit has this one indispensable genuine mark then: it is Christ-centred — it is designed to exalt Christ and glorify him in the minds and hearts of men and women and boys and girls. As the great nineteenth-century Baptist preacher Charles Haddon Spurgeon (1834-1892) once put it:

> If we do not make the Lord Jesus glorious; if we do not lift him high in the esteem of men, if we do not labour to make him King of kings, and Lord of lords; we shall not have the Holy Spirit with us. Vain will be rhetoric, music, architecture, energy, and social status: if our one design be not to magnify the Lord Jesus, we shall work alone and work in vain.[2]

Or as he said it more quaintly in a sermon preached in July 1884: 'the Holy Spirit always keeps sweet company with Jesus Christ'.[3]

THE NEW TESTAMENT: A CHRIST-CENTRED BOOK

Can a person love the Lord Jesus too much? Is there any limit to one's heart-devotion to this Person? A discerning reader of the New Testament, which has been breathed into existence by the Spirit of God, can answer both of these questions quite easily: absolutely not.

The New Testament is filled from start to finish with ardent devotion to Jesus Christ. He is declared to be the fountain of all knowledge and wisdom (Col. 2:3), the One who sustains every particle of the universe and every fibre of our being (Col. 1:16-17; Heb. 1:3). He is set forth as the supreme reason for living (2 Cor. 5:9). Gazing into his face one can see perfectly and without the slightest distortion the very glory of God (Heb. 1:3). He owns angels (Matt. 24:31), and they know well their Master and are not afraid to bow in worship before him (Heb. 1:6). To him belongs the incredible privilege of bestowing the Spirit of God upon whom he wishes (Acts 2:33). And his name is supremely precious, because by no other name can sinners be saved (Acts 4:12).

Due to all this Jesus is worthy to be worshipped in the identical manner as God the Father (Rev. 5). No praise, no depth of adoration is too much to give him. He is worthy of all of our being's devotion for he is God, the great God come to earth to lay down his life for sinners (John 1:1,14; Rom. 9:5; Titus 2:13). Not to love him and to be devoted him without reservation is to dishonour God and to grieve the Spirit in his Christ-centred ministry. It is the Father's great delight that all honour the Son in this way. Little wonder that as Paul wraps up his great letter to the churches in Ephesus, he can declare, 'Grace be with all who love our Lord Jesus Christ with love incorruptible' (Eph. 6:24).

Outside of Scripture such extravagant love for Christ is well captured in the nineteenth-century hymn, 'Jesus, wondrous Saviour'. Its author, D. A. McGregor (1847-1890), was the principal of Toronto Baptist College when he wrote it, and it came from a heart aflame with devotion for the Saviour. Its first and last two stanzas run thus — and notice how the second to last stanza contains a clear allusion to Colossians 1:17:

> Jesus, wondrous Saviour!
> Christ, of kings the King!
> Angels fall before Thee
> Prostrate, worshipping.
> Fairest they confess Thee
> In the Heavens above,
> We would sing Thee fairest
> Here in hymns of love.
>
> Life is death if severed
> From Thy throbbing heart.

Death with life abundant
At Thy touch would start.
Worlds and men and angels
All consist in Thee:
Yet Thou camest to us
In humility.

Jesus! all perfections
Rise and end in Thee;
Brightness of God's glory
Thou, eternally.
Favour'd beyond measure
They Thy face who see;
May we, gracious Saviour,
Share this ecstasy.[4]

MOSES — A CHRIST-CENTRED MAN

Consider the testimony about Moses in Hebrews 11:23-26:

> By faith Moses, when he was born, was hidden for three
> months by his parents, because they saw that the child was
> beautiful, and they were not afraid of the king's edict. By faith,
> Moses, when he was grown up, refused to be called the son
> of Pharaoh's daughter, choosing rather to be mistreated with
> the people of God than to enjoy the fleeting pleasures of sin.
> He considered the reproach of Christ greater wealth than
> the treasures of Egypt, for he was looking to the reward.

The author of Hebrews tells us little about Moses' early years
apart from the fact that at the time of his birth his parents hid him
and that he was a beautiful infant. From Exodus 1, we learn that
the Egyptian Pharaoh had passed an edict requiring the Hebrew
midwives to slay the male babies of their race when they were
born. He was afraid that the Hebrews would outstrip the Egyptians in population growth and eventually come to dominate the

Egyptians in the Nile Delta. Moses' parents, Amram and Jochebed (Exod. 6:20), though, feared God and showed themselves to be people of faith (Heb. 11:23). So they disobeyed the wicked edict of Pharaoh and hid Moses when he was born.

The time came, however, when they could hide him no longer. So they placed him in an 'ark' (and the same word is used here in the Exodus account as in the Genesis account about Noah), an 'ark of bulrushes, daubed' with 'bitumen and pitch' (Exod. 2:3), and by faith placed him in the Nile River. They acted in faith, for they trusted that God would take care of their son. In the providence of God, Pharaoh's daughter came down to the Nile, and saw the tiny infant adrift on the water. She drew him from the water and took him into the royal household. She proceeded to adopt him and raise him as her own child.

And it was she who named him Moses (Exod. 2:10). Presumably his parents had also named him before this, but that name has not come down to us. As John Owen says in his massive seven-volume commentary on Hebrews: this name Moses 'is that which God would have him use, as a perpetual remembrance of his deliverance, when he was in a helpless condition'.[5] So Moses, the child of humble Hebrew parents, was raised in line to the throne of Egypt. As Hebrews 11 puts it, he was raised as the 'son of Pharaoh's daughter' and so possessed 'the treasures of Egypt'. In other words, as Owen writes, 'the secular interest, power, glory, honour, and wealth' of Egypt's royal palace were his.[6]

When Moses grew up in the court of Pharaoh, the Egyptian Empire had been flourishing for well over a thousand years. Many of the pyramids, for example, had been standing at that point for anywhere between 600 and 800 years. They spoke eloquently of Egypt's great wealth and earthly might. Outside of Egypt, the Pharaonic kingdom was known and feared as a great world power. When the Pharaoh gave orders to his mighty army, his chariots and warriors went out to make war and conquest, and the powers of the Ancient Near East trembled.

In the thousand years before Moses was born Egypt had known

a number of major ups and downs. In Moses' day it was enjoying another period of wealth, prosperity and power. Queen Hatshepsut, for instance, who reigned over Egypt for about fifteen years between roughly 1473 B.C. and 1458 B.C. — which is only a few years before the Exodus[7] — had brought great prosperity and wealth to Egypt. In the Royal Ontario Museum in Toronto, for instance, there is a mosaic that tells the story of a great trading venture that Queen Hatshepsut sent to what is modern Somalia to bring back ivory, and gold and precious spices to Egypt.[8] In fact, Egypt was famous for its gold. For example, when the grave of Tutankhamun (died *c.*1327 B.C.) was discovered in 1922, it was found that thousands of pounds of gold had been used in his grave furniture, mummy mask, coffin and jewellery. His 'inner coffin alone contained over three thousand pounds of gold'.[9]

Then, the pleasures that would have been available to Moses in the Egyptian royal family were vast. By tradition, Pharaoh's court was a place of pomp and luxury. Pharaoh was regarded as a living god, and so his court had to reflect his splendour. There was lavish entertainment and all that one could desire. Hebrews 11:25 mentions these ultimately fleeting 'pleasures'. From Acts 7:22 we learn that Moses also had all of the intellectual pleasures he could desire: 'Moses was learned in all the wisdom of the Egyptians.'

Yet, Moses renounced all of this. The verb that is used in Hebrews 11:24 to indicate this — 'refused' (*ernesato*) — is particularly strong. The verb is used, for example, in Matthew 10:33 of denying Christ before other human beings and in 1 John 2:22 of the Antichrist who denies God the Father and the Son. All of his privileges, all of his pleasures as an Egyptian prince, all of the wealth and power, all of the status — Moses renounced all of it. And he did not do this when he was a man in his late teens or twenties, when such things might be easily given up. But he did it when he was a mature man in his late thirties and he was nearing forty, an age, when, as John Owen says, such things as power and wealth and status 'give the greatest gust and relish...unto the minds of men'.[10] Why did he do it?

Well, our first clue to the answer to this question is that it was 'by faith' Moses 'refused to be called the son of Pharaoh's daughter' (Heb. 11:24). According to Hebrews 11:1 — which introduces this chapter on the heroes of faith — 'faith is the assurance of things hoped for, the conviction of things not seen'. It was his faith in God that gave Moses the power to leave behind forever the pleasures of the Egyptian court.

Many of those pleasures were, of course, not wrong in themselves. For has not God given humanity all things richly to enjoy (1 Tim. 6:17)? But these pleasures that God gives become sin when they come between a man and God. When they prevent people from following God wholeheartedly, then they are sin. Moreover, none of these pleasures were worthy of being Moses' heart-treasure. None of them, not even the best of them, were worthy of being the ultimate goal of Moses' life and ambitions — nor ours for that matter!

Faith enabled Moses to see two things very clearly. First, it was by faith that Moses perceived that the Israelites — certainly not a glittering group of people but, rather, humble slaves, a 'company of brick-makers', to use John Owen words[11] — were none other than the people of the living God. Men have always been desirous of belonging to the glitterati — the rich and famous and powerful. But God's people, no matter their faults and problems, no matter their failings and sins, are, in the words of John Owen, 'ten thousand times more honourable than any other society of men in the world'.[12] When we are tempted to complain about the church to which we belong, we need to remember who they are — they are God's people. In other words, there can be no loving God without loving his people, without esteeming their society the best of all societies. 'We know', the apostle John says in 1 John 3:14, 'that we have passed out of death into life, because we love the brothers.' So Moses chose to suffer with God's people; he gave up all of the privileges and power of Pharaoh's court to suffer with the people of God.

But we still have yet to come to the spring, the taproot, the heart of Moses' action. Read on in Hebrews 11:26. First, notice what the text does *not* say. It does not say that 'he considered Christ to be greater than the treasures of Egypt'. No — it was being *reproached* for the sake of Christ that he considered a much greater treasure than all the treasures of Egypt. When Moses compared in his mind the treasures of the Egyptian court along-side suffering for the sake of Christ, it was suffering for the sake of Christ that he esteemed to be the greater treasure. The context in which this verse was written needs to be recalled at this point. Some of the recipients were on the verge of drawing back from a whole-hearted following of their Lord (see Heb. 10:32-39). Lest they be ashamed of Christ, the author of Hebrews reminds them that Moses had faced a similar situation and they need to imitate his love for Christ, come what may.

But, someone might read these words and think to himself: Christ had not yet come when Moses made this choice. Moses lived nearly 1,500 years before the birth of Jesus Christ. Yet, it was by faith that Moses was enabled to look down the corridors of history and see the Messiah, the Christ, coming from this afflicted 'company of brick-makers'. And it was out of longing for the Christ that Moses was willing to throw in his lot with the people of God and share in their sufferings. It was because his heart was aflame with possessing the One who is the greatest of all treasures in this entire universe, Jesus the Christ, that he was more than willing to give up all of the treasures of Egypt. Fifteen centuries later, on the Mount of Transfiguration he would gaze upon the face of the One for whom he gave up all things and know it was worth it all (Mark 9:2-8). True New Testament spirituality is here typified by the Old Testament figure of Moses. It is ruled by a unquenchable love for Christ and an unstoppable desire to see him glorified.

This hymn of Ann Griffiths, whom we met in the first chapter,[13] beautifully expresses this absolute of New Testament spirituality:

Let my days be wholly given
    Jesus' blood to glorify,

Calm to rest beneath his shadow,
  At his feet to live and die,
Love the cross, and bear it daily,
  ('Tis the cross my Husband bore,)
Gaze with joy upon his Person,
  And unceasingly adore.[14]

'The burned-over place'

CHAPTER FOUR

A cross-centred
SPIRITUALITY

One of the most moving stories in English literature is Charles Dickens' *A Tale of Two Cities*, set during the time of the French Revolution in the 1790s. The hero of the story, Sydney Carton, an English lawyer, adores Lucie Manette, the daughter of a French émigré. In the course of the story, however, Lucie gets married to a man named Charles Darnay, the nephew of a French aristocrat and one who is also taking refuge in England from the terror in France. Upon a return trip to France, Darnay is captured by French revolutionaries and sentenced to die on the guillotine. Carton, who is a striking look-alike of Darnay, arranges to have Darnay drugged and smuggled out of prison the night before he is to die. Darnay returns to England, to his wife Lucie and to his new home. Carton meanwhile disguises himself as Darnay, takes his place, and is led out to execution the following day. As he ascends the scaffold, Carton thinks of what he has done: 'I see the lives for which I lay down my life, peaceful, useful, prosperous and happy, in that England which I shall see no more. ...It is a far, far better thing that I do, than I have ever done; it is far, far better rest that I go to, than I have ever known.'[1]

Carton's sacrifice of his life for Darnay and for Lucie is undoubtedly a very heroic act, and could well serve as an inspiring example of selfless love. In the history of the church there have actually been some who have understood the death of Christ primarily in this way. For them Christ's death is a heroic act, similar to that of a martyr.

CHRIST'S DEATH AS AN EXAMPLE

These authors take their cue from a few New Testament texts, like Philippians 2:5-8 and 1 Peter 2:21-24, that focus on the cross as an example of how to deal with suffering and persecution. In the passage from 1 Peter we are explicitly told that on the cross Jesus Christ set his followers an example of patient suffering. He became the pattern of all who would believe in him, showing them how they should behave in difficult and trying circumstances.

It was Liberal theologians in the late-nineteenth and early-twentieth centuries, seeking to advance an agenda of removing all traces of the supernatural from Scripture, who frequently pictured Christ's death as the supreme instance of utterly selfless love. A good example in this regard is the thinking of L. H. Marshall (1882-1953),[2] whose teaching at McMaster University, Ontario, Canada, in the late 1920s was extremely controversial. Marshall saw the crucifixion of Christ as the supreme example of divine love, but not as a vicarious punishment for the sins of his people.[3] Christ's death thus became equivalent to that of a martyr.[4] The leading opponent of Marshall's teaching on this and other things was the conservative pastor of Jarvis Street Baptist Church in Toronto, T. T. Shields (1873-1955).[5] After two years of struggle with McMaster University's administration over Marshall's teaching, Shields decided to found his own seminary, Toronto Baptist Seminary. Taking the *New Hampshire Confession of Faith* (1833) as the model for the new seminary's statement of

faith, Shields made the following assertion regarding the death
of Christ:

> by His death [Christ] made a full and expiatory atonement
> for our sins…that…consisted not in setting us an example
> by His death as a martyr, but was the voluntary substitution
> of Himself in the sinner's place, bearing the penalty of God's
> Holy Law, the Just dying for the unjust, Christ, the Lord,
> bearing our sins in His own body on the tree…[6]

The final clauses of this statement are drawn from 1 Peter 3:18
and 1 Peter 2:24 and are rightly taken to indicate that Christ's
death is completely different from all the heroic deaths in the
annals of history and literature.

THE SINLESSNESS OF THE SAVIOUR

Let us look at 1 Peter 3:18 in more detail. Here Peter affirms,
first of all, that 'Christ also suffered once *for sins*.'[7] Whose sins?
Certainly not his own, for Scripture is unequivocal in its assertion
that Christ never sinned.

As we look at Christ's life as it is recorded in the four Gospels,
there is not one incident to which we can point and say, 'Look, a
sin.' We never hear him asking for forgiveness, from God or from
man. In fact, he can pointedly state in John 8:46: 'Which one of
you convicts me of sin?' This question bespeaks a conscience that
is absolutely clear of sin and in utterly unbroken fellowship with
God the Father. During the moments leading up to his passion,
Christ makes a similar declaration when he states that 'the ruler
of this world is coming. He has no claim on me' (John 14:30).
The devil has no claim upon Christ, for Christ had never sinned.
Again, listen to the testimony of the repentant criminal on the
cross (Luke 23:33-41). This man recognized that he was receiving
the just penalty for his crimes; but Christ had 'done nothing
wrong' (verse 41). He was completely innocent.[8]
Or again, meditate on 2 Corinthians 5:20-21. Christ 'knew

(*gnonta*) no sin' (verse 21). In both classical and koiné Greek, the latter being the language of the New Testament, there are two verbs that can be translated 'to know'. The one, *oida*, generally means to have possession of knowledge and is used to describe complete and full knowledge. The other, *ginōskō*, usually depicts the acquisition of knowledge and represents that knowledge as incomplete and in the process of development. While the apostle Paul does not always make a definite distinction between these two verbs, of the 103 times where he employs *oida*, 90 are used with the above distinction in mind. And of the 50 occurrences of *ginōskō*, 32 are used with the distinct meaning of this verb. In 2 Corinthians 5:21 Paul appears to be using this latter verb with its distinctive meaning. In other words, Christ did not gain or acquire a knowledge of human sinfulness by overt acts of sin. Sin was something completely foreign to his life and heart. How unlike us! For us, sin is something we have always known; not a day has gone by in our lives when sin has not been present with us. All of us can look back and remember times when we have warmly entertained sin, and made it welcome in the innermost recesses of our hearts and lives. But not Christ! He 'knew no sin'.

But we must go further and affirm that the sinlessness of Jesus also means that Christ did not possess a nature bent and warped by the presence of sin. In Christ there was no *inherent* sin. 1 Peter 1:19 affirms that he was 'without blemish or spot', that is, blameless and free from vice. 1 John 3:5 asserts that 'in him there is no sin'. Hebrews 7:26 describes him as one 'holy, innocent, unstained, separated from sinners'. In other words, Christ had no inner compulsion or desire to engage in sin. He always delighted in the will of God and in holiness. As he said in John 4:34: 'My food is to do the will of him who sent me and to accomplish his work.'

The Scriptures, therefore, deny not only the presence of sinful thinking and acts in the incarnate Christ, but also, in the words of H. P. Liddon (1829-1890), the Victorian High Anglican, 'any ultimate roots and sources of sin, of any propensities or inclinations, however latent and rudimentary, towards sin'. The words of James 1:14-15, which indicate that every man and woman is tempted to sin by an inner inclination towards sin, do not apply to Christ. It is our lusts that motivate and draw us into sin. But Christ knows absolutely nothing of this. To say that Christ had sinful inclinations is to assert nothing less than that Christ himself was in need of a Saviour! In other words, Christ *could* not sin.

What then of his temptations, were they real? We read of these in the Gospel accounts and in a passage like Hebrews 4:15: 'We do not have a high priest who is unable to sympathize with our weaknesses, but one who in every respect has been tempted as we are, yet without sin.' Christ knows our frame intimately, for he has stood where we stand, 'yet without sin'. Against us, who are so very used to sinning, Satan the tempter does not have to use all of his demonic craft to convince us to engage in sin. But against the sinless Saviour he threw the entirety of his energy and strength. The forces of temptation that Satan blew against Christ were of hurricane intensity, so unlike the winds that bother us, yet he did not yield to them.

Returning then to the question: for whose sins then did Christ die? It can only be *our* sins. Peter had already made this point earlier in the letter. In 1 Peter 2:24, the apostle says, Christ 'bore *our* sins in his body on the tree', that is the cross (italics added). Peter, therefore, is not talking merely about the sins of those who opposed Jesus in the days of his earthly ministry and who eventually crucified him. Peter is talking about *his own* sins and *your* sins and *my* sins.[9]

'THE BURNED-OVER PLACE'

To illustrate what Christ has done for his people Paul Zahl gives the following account of a duck hunter and his friend in a wide-open barren stretch of land in southeastern Georgia.

> Far away on the horizon he noticed a cloud of smoke. Soon he could hear the sound of crackling. A wind came up, and he realized the terrible truth: a brushfire was advancing his

way. It was moving so fast that he and his friend could not outrun it. The hunter began to rifle through his pockets. Then he emptied all the contents of his knapsack. He soon found what he was looking for — a book of matches. To his friend's amazement, he pulled out a match and struck it. He lit a small fire around the two of them. Soon they were standing in a circle of blackened earth, waiting for the fire to come. They did not have to wait long. They covered their mouths with their handkerchiefs and braced themselves. The fire came near — and swept [by]...them. But they were completely unhurt. They weren't even touched. Fire would not pass where fire had passed.

Zahl goes on to note that divine judgement for sin is like the brushfire. Sinful human beings cannot escape it. But if they stand in the burned-over place, where punishment has already been meted out, then they will not be hurt. 'The death of Christ', Zahl triumphantly declares, 'is the burned-over place.' There, and there alone, is there safety from the fire of God's judgement. There, and there alone, is there mercy and forgiveness of sin.[10]

DRAWING NEAR TO GOD THROUGH THE CROSS

Christ died, Peter states in 1 Peter 3:18, that 'he might bring us to God'. The inference of such a statement is that sin keeps human beings far from God.[11] Sin erects barriers between man and God (Eph. 2:11-18). It makes men and women strangers, and even enemies, of God. Thus, the Scriptures speak of the death of Christ as a propitiation, a turning-aside of the righteous anger, of God against human sin (Rom. 3:25). Christ's death reconciles human beings to God and turns aside his righteous wrath. 'Those who commit themselves to Christ and to the work which He has done for them in His passion, are now able to draw near to God and to live in His peace' and his presence.[12]

What does all of this mean for Christian spirituality? First, spiritual access to God in prayer, in worship and in fellowship is not something that we should take lightly or take for granted. Access to God is the greatest of human privileges, one that has been purchased at an indescribable cost: the death of the Lord Jesus, sinless man and very God. As Peter tells his readers in 1 Peter 1:18-19, you were 'ransomed from your futile ways...with the precious blood of Christ, like that of a lamb without blemish or spot.'[13]

Second, there is no other way to know God spiritually and to worship him but through Christ and him crucified. Thus, crucicentrism, this passionate focus on the crucified Christ, is a central feature of any spirituality claiming to be biblical and evangelical.[14] As British historian David Bebbington has noted, evangelicals have historically 'placed at the centre of their theological scheme the doctrine of the cross — the atoning work of Jesus Christ in his death'.[15]

We live in a culture that encourages a pluralistic attitude towards God and religion. All religions, it tells us, are equal. All religions, it would have us believe, are pathways to God. It tells us that to think there is only one way to God is rigid and narrow. But this pluralistic perspective is a complete denial of what Peter is saying in 1 Peter 3. Peter and the rest of the Scriptures tell us there is only *one* way to God and that is through Christ and his cross. He died 'that he might bring us to God'. If other ways to God were possible, Christ would not have had to die. But other ways were not possible! Christ had to die to satisfy God's justice and in mercy 'bring us to God'.

A WORD ON JUSTIFICATION

At the cross God deals decisively with our sins. All of our sins are imputed to Christ. When we believe this, we are brought into a living union with Christ and made right with God. And in this union, something else is imputed: the righteousness of Christ is imputed to the person who puts his or her trust (*fiducia*) in Christ.

This was the decisive discovery of Martin Luther (1483-1546), the pathfinder of the Reformation. Prior to this discovery Luther had come to see all too clearly that he was a sinner who could

never obtain the righteousness God that demanded in his law, and
that therefore one day he would be bound to face the withering
wrath of God, for God is a holy God who abhors sin. By this
discovery of salvation solely through Christ's death apart from
his works, Luther realized that salvation was not at all a matter
of his attaining the perfect standard of righteousness that God
demanded. Rather, simply and by faith, he had to rely upon Christ's
righteousness. For Christ alone among men and women has never
sinned, he alone has lived a life of perfect righteousness and he
alone had perfectly fulfilled the law and its righteous demands.[16]
Luther's discovery was that salvation from God's wrath was to be
found by simple trust in Christ's death for sinners. At the cross
Christ takes all responsibility for a believer's sins — past, present
and future — and to the one who truly believes, God imputes (or,
reckons as the believer's own) Christ's righteousness.

What Luther realized was that salvation 'was not a matter of
Martin and his righteousness, but of God and His Righteousness,
not a matter of Martin's work but God's work'. Luther realized that
biblical Christianity was not about so-called works of merit and the
mediæval structure of spirituality with its pilgrimages, fast days,
reception of the Mass, etc., but a simple surrender in faith to God's
unique saving work in Jesus Christ and him crucified. Again, here is
Luther describing what justification by faith alone means:

> I, Dr Martin Luther, the unworthy evangelist of the Lord
> Jesus Christ, thus think and thus affirm: — that this article,
> viz., that faith alone, without works, justifies before God,
> can never be overthrown, for…Christ alone, the Son of
> God, died for our sins, but if He alone takes away our sins,
> then men, with all their works, are to be excluded from all
> concurrence in procuring the pardon of sin and justification.
> Nor can I embrace Christ otherwise than by faith alone; He
> cannot be apprehended by works. But if faith, before works
> follow, apprehends the Redeemer, it is undoubtedly true that
> faith alone, before works, and without works, appropriates

the benefits of redemption, which is no other than justification, or deliverance from sin. This is our doctrine; so the Holy Spirit teaches the whole Christian Church. In this, by the grace of God, will we stand fast. Amen.[17]

Notice what Luther is saying here: we are justified by faith alone, faith in Christ's death for sinners. Our works do not enter the picture at all when it comes to being made right with God. Thus 'faith' itself is not to be considered 'a work'. The faith we exercise is itself a gift from God, a creation of the Holy Spirit. It is the Holy Spirit who enables sinners to accept God's justifying work on their behalf.[18]

And in the final analysis, our faith only justifies because it lays hold of Christ, who, in the words of American theologian Michael Horton, is 'inexhaustible in riches of righteousness'.[19] Our faith is often weak, but it is the unconquerable strength of Christ's righteousness, not the strength of our faith, that keeps us in a right standing before God. Or to use Luther's own words:

> I believe that it is not of my own reason or my own strength that I believe in Jesus Christ my Lord. It is the Holy Spirit that by the Gospel has called me, with his gifts has enlightened me, through genuine faith has sanctified and sustained me, just as he calls, gathers together, enlightens, sanctifies and sustains, by Jesus Christ, in true and proper faith, all Christendom.[20]

'Our only infallible rule'

CHAPTER FIVE

A spirituality
OF THE WORD

In 1778 Benjamin Francis (1734-1799), a Welsh Baptist minister who pastored in the south-west of England for most of his life, had occasion to write to some fellow believers in an association of Baptist churches. In his letter he laid out for them what is a foundational element of evangelical spirituality:

> We earnestly beseech you carefully to guard against all pernicious errors in doctrine, experience and practice, and to bring all your religious sentiments, feelings, and actions, to the unerring test of God's word, our only infallible rule in matters of religion. Buy the truth, cost what it will, and sell it not for all the world.[1]

Notice the affirmation here: the Scriptures are inerrant and therefore a sure guide for the Christian's doctrine and world-view, as well as his experience and lifestyle.

A similar Word-centred emphasis can be found in a letter written in 1835 by a young man named Adam Murray, a native of New Brunswick who had come to what was then called Upper Canada, now known as Ontario, to carve a living out for himself as a schoolteacher and possibly also as a farmer. A godly young Presbyterian, he had hoped at one time to study for pastoral ministry. But, for some reason, possibly financial, this had not proven possible. Writing home to his mother after he had been in Upper Canada for a while he told her of the blessings of the land in which he was now living and how anyone who wanted to work hard could prosper in any of the new settlements springing up throughout southern Ontario. But then he turned to what he considered the greatest blessing of all: 'we have the inestimable privilege', he wrote, of hearing 'the preaching of the Gospel, twice every five months'.

Murray was not being sarcastic nor was he complaining. The context in which he makes this statement indicates that he is deeply thankful that amid all the hardships of pioneer life he could hear the Word of God as the gospel was preached. He seems to have counted the hearing of God's Word as the greatest privilege of his life. Murray never became a pastor or preacher of the gospel, though he did become an elder in the Presbyterian Church. His obituary records that at the time of his death he was widely famed for his wealth of Scripture knowledge and understanding of reformed theology.[2]

This one line from a letter Murray wrote over 170 years ago as well the opening quote from Benjamin Francis are good reminders of the way Christians have thought about the distinctness and uniqueness of the book we call the Bible.

THE 'WORD OF GOD'

Christians often describe the Bible as the 'Word of God'. In this we are simply following the Bible's own self-description.[3] When we make this declaration about the Bible we are affirming that ultimately it has God for its origin. Yes, there is no doubt that the various books that make up the Bible were written by human beings like us. Different men from vastly different cultures wrote it over a period of more than 1,500 years. Consider 2 John 12 in this regard, where John refers to two of the essential tools for writing in the ancient world: papyrus and ink. The Bible thus has all the features and earmarks of any other human book and can be studied as such. One can examine the different characteristics and emphases of the various human writers in the Bible, investigate when and why their individual contributions to the Bible were written and, in general, study them as one would study other ancient writers. But, and this is utterly critical to affirm, the Bible also has God for its author.

A time-honoured proof text for this dual authorship of the Bible is found in 2 Peter 1:20-21. In the immediate context Peter has been assuring his readers that what has been made known to them of 'the power and coming of our Lord Jesus Christ' were not 'fables' or myths 'cleverly devised' by himself or the other apostles. He first offers them the testimony of those who actually saw the unveiled glory of Christ. Here Peter appears to be thinking of his own experience on the Mount of Transfiguration or possibly one of the times that he saw the risen Christ. But then Peter makes the assertion that he and his readers have better testimony than such dramatic eyewitness evidence. They have the 'prophetic word' (verse 19), that is, they have the Old Testament Scriptures. These Scriptures themselves are surer than any personal experience. Alluding to a verse like Psalm 119:105 — 'Your word is a lamp to my feet and a light to my path' — Peter forthrightly declares that it is the Scriptures which will provide light in the midst of the murky darkness of this world until Christ returns.

And why can they trust the Scriptures? Because, Peter writes, 'no prophecy was ever produced by the will of man, but men spoke from God as they were carried along by the Holy Spirit' (2 Peter 1:21). There are at least three noteworthy points about this text. First, there is the clear assertion that the Scriptures were written by men — human authors were definitely and vitally involved.

Second, these human writers were not on their own when it came to the composition and recording of their thoughts and ideas. Ultimately the Bible — neither the Old Testament that

Peter has in immediate view here nor the New Testament, of which 2 Peter forms a part — does not originate in the initiative and design of human beings. Rather, it has been written by men 'carried along by the Holy Spirit'.

Finally, the word translated here by 'carried along' or 'moved' should not be taken to mean that the human author was forced to speak against his will or that he lost his own self-control. Notice the careful way that Peter expresses it. At the same time as they were being 'moved' by the Holy Spirit, the authors of Scripture were speaking. The minds and wills of these human authors were fully engaged as they wrote. In some cases — for example, Luke in Acts — they did extensive research before they wrote. Moreover, when they wrote they used personal idiosyncrasies of style, distinctive vocabulary patterns and idioms of speech. This process, which we call inspiration, entailed neither an abnormal state of mind on the part of the writer as he wrote nor an obliteration of his personality; nor does it mean that he became a mere dictation machine. But all the time it was the Holy Spirit who was bearing these men along so that which would eventually result as the end product of their writing was fully in accord with God's purpose and desires.

Inspiration can thus be described as a concursive action. As J. I. Packer explains this unique literary phenomenon: 'We are to think of the Spirit's inspiring activity…as *concursive*; that is, as exercised in, through and by means of the writers' own activity, in such a way that their thinking and writing was *both* free and spontaneous on their part *and* divinely elicited and controlled, and what they wrote was not only their own work but also God's work.'[4]

THE SUFFICIENCY OF SCRIPTURE

To talk of the Scriptures as the inspired Word of God is also to affirm the absolute sufficiency of the Bible in all that it addresses. Paul, can write thus in his final letter to Timothy, at a point where he is convinced that he is about to pass from this world to the next:

Continue in what you have learned and have firmly believed, knowing from whom you learned it and how from childhood you have been acquainted with the sacred writings, which are able to make you wise for salvation through faith in Christ Jesus. All Scripture is breathed out by God (*theopneustos*) and profitable for teaching, for reproof, for correction and for training in righteousness, that the man of God may be competent, equipped for every good work (2 Tim. 3:14-17).

Here the apostle affirms that the Scriptures are altogether sufficient to make people knowledgeable in doctrine and 'thoroughly equipped for every good work'. The Scriptures are so designed to help them steer clear of heresy and a lifestyle that is not in accord with the gospel. Now, why can they do these things? Because of one simple fact — they are 'God-breathed' (*theopneustos*).

By using this particular word, Paul is unequivocally declaring that the Scriptures — both the Old Testament that was already in a written form and the New Testament that was at that very moment in the process of being inscripturated — are the product of the creative work of God the Holy Spirit. Note the oblique reference to the Spirit, the Holy Breath (*pneuma*) of God, in the termination of the word 'God-breathed' (*pneustos*). In the final analysis, Paul asserts, Scripture — all of the words as they were originally given — must be seen as originating in the mind of God. While men were indeed employed as the means by which the Scriptures have come to us, yet their ultimate author is none other than the Spirit of God. It is for this reason that they can be trusted to achieve all of God's purposes. In other words: the Scriptures are entirely trustworthy because of the One who stands behind them as their author.

RESPONDING TO GOD'S WORD

How then are we to respond to these facts? Well, because the Bible has God for its ultimate author, we approach it as we approach no other book:

- With the Lord Jesus, we affirm God's Word to be the truth (John 17:17)
- We recognize its authority as coming from God (1 Thess. 4:1-8)
- We listen to it with reverence (1 Thess. 2:13)
- We submit to its teaching (Isa. 66:2)
- We are confident that the Holy Spirit will bring it alive for us and help us to understand it (Eph. 6:17; Heb. 4:12)
- We hunger for it (Jer. 15:16; Ps. 19:7-10)
- We affirm it to be our guide for all of life (Ps. 119:105).

A MODEL TO PONDER: THE WORD-CENTRED LIFE OF WILLIAM TYNDALE [5]

In 1994 the British Library paid the equivalent of well over two million dollars (over one million pounds) for a book which Dr Brian Lang, the chief executive of the Library at the time, described as 'one of the most important acquisitions in our 240 year history'.[6] The book? A copy of the New Testament. Of course, it was not just *any* copy. In fact, there are only two other New Testaments like this one in existence. One of these copies is in the library of St Paul's Cathedral, London, and is lacking seventy-one of its pages. The other copy has only recently come to light in the Biblesammlung at the Württembergische Landesbibliothek in Stuttgart.[7] What is especially noteworthy about this latter copy is the fact that it contains Tyndale's title-page which the British Library copy does not have. It reads thus (the original English is retained):

> The newe Testament as it was written and caused to be written by them which herde yt. To whom also oure saveuor Christ Jesus commaunded that they shulde preache it unto al creatures.[8]

The New Testament that the British Museum purchased was

lodged for many years in the library of the oldest Baptist seminary in the world, Bristol Baptist College. This New Testament
had been bequeathed to the College by Andrew Gifford (1700-
1784), a well-known London Baptist minister in his day. Gifford
had purchased it in 1776 from a certain John White, who had
in turn bought it from the bibliographer Joseph Ames (1689-
1759). The latter had come to own it through a bookseller by
the name of Thomas Osborne who had sold it to Ames for a
mere 15 shillings.

It was printed in the German town of Worms (pronounced
'warms') on the press of Peter Schoeffer in 1526 and is known as
the Tyndale New Testament. The first printed New Testament to
be translated into English out of the original Greek, it is indeed an
invaluable book. Its translator, after whom it is named, was William
Tyndale (d.1536). Of his overall significance in the history of the
church, the article on him in the famous eleventh edition of the
Encyclopædia Britannica justifiably states that he was 'one of the
greatest forces of the English Reformation', a man whose writings
'helped to shape the thought of the Puritan party in England'.[9]

In strong contrast to mediæval Roman Catholicism, where piety
was focused on the proper performance of certain external rituals,
Tyndale, like the rest of the Reformers, emphasized that at the
heart of Christianity was faith, which presupposed an understanding of what was believed. Knowledge of the Scriptures, and that
in the vernacular (i.e. English language), was therefore essential
in Tyndale's mind to Christian spirituality and any growth in
Christian maturity.

Tyndale's determination to give the people of England the
Word of God so gripped him that from the mid-1520s till his
martyrdom in 1536 his life was directed to this sole end. What
lay behind this single-minded vision was a particular view of
God's Word. In his 'Prologue' to his translation of Genesis, which
he wrote in 1530, Tyndale could state: 'the Scripture is a light,
and sheweth us the true way, both what to do and what to hope
for; and a defence from all error, and a comfort in adversity that

we despair not, and feareth us in prosperity that we sin not'.[10] Despite opposition from church authorities and the martyrdom of Tyndale in 1536, the Word of God became absolutely central to the English Reformation. As David Daniell has noted in what is the definitive biography of Tyndale, it was Tyndale's translation that made the English people a 'People of the Book'.[11]

The Reformation thus involved a major shift of emphasis in the cultivation of Christian spirituality. Mediæval Roman Catholicism had majored on symbols and images as the means for cultivating spirituality. The Reformation, coming as it did at the time of the invention of the printing press, turned back to the biblical emphasis on 'words' as the primary vehicle of cultivating spirituality, both spoken words and written words and, in particular, the words of the Bible.

Evangelicalism has been strong when it has likewise sought to cultivate a spirituality that is first and foremost centred in the Scriptures. Of course, we face challenges in this regard. There are those in our day who assert that words are no longer adequate. We need images and drama, they say. But if one traces the history of Christian spirituality it is frequent to find that those who asserted a spirituality of the Word were also criticized and verbally attacked.

THE PURITAN INTERFACE OF SPIRIT AND WORD

Consider, for instance, the Puritan spirituality of the Word that was challenged by radicals to their left. There were the Muggletonians, founded by Lodowick Muggleton (1609-1698) and his cousin John Reeve (1608-1658), who believed that they were the two witnesses of Revelation 11:3-6 and who denied the doctrine of the trinity, rejected preaching and prayer, and argued that the revelation given to Muggleton and Reeve was God's final word to mankind. Even more dangerous to the Puritan cause were the Quakers, in some ways the counterpart to the charismatic movement of the modern era.

The Quaker movement, which would become a major alternative to Puritanism, started in the late 1640s when George Fox (1624-1691), a shoemaker and part-time shepherd, began to win converts to a perspective on the Christian faith that rejected much of orthodox Puritan theology.[12] Fox and the early Quakers proclaimed the possibility of salvation for all humanity, and urged men and women to turn to the light within them to find salvation. We 'call All men to look to the Light within their own consciences', wrote Samuel Fisher (1605-1665), a General Baptist turned Quaker; 'by the leadings of that Light… they may come to God, and work out their Salvation'.[13] This emphasis on the light within, which the Quakers variously called the indwelling Christ or Spirit, often led them to elevate it above the Scriptures.

With the Quakers, there was a deep conviction that the Spirit was speaking in them as he had spoken in the apostles. In practice, this often led to an elevation of their experience of the indwelling Spirit over the Scriptures. Thus, when some Baptists in Huntingdonshire and Cambridgeshire became Quakers and declared that the 'light in their consciences was the rule they desire to walk by', not the Scriptures, they were simply expressing what was implicit in the entire Quaker movement.[14]

Isaac Penington the Younger (1616-1679) is one early Quaker author who illustrates this tendency to make the indwelling Spirit rather than the Scriptures the touchstone and final authority for thought and practice. Converted to Quakerism in 1658 after hearing George Fox preach the previous year, Penington became an important figure in the movement. In the words of J. W. Frost, Penington 'remains a prime example of the intellectual sophistication of the second generation of Quaker converts'.[15] In a letter that he wrote a fellow Quaker by the name of Nathanael Stonar in 1670, Penington told his correspondent that one of the main differences between themselves and other 'professors' was 'concerning *the rule*'. While the latter asserted that the Scriptures were the rule by which men and women ought to direct their lives and thinking, Penington was convinced that the indwelling Spirit of life is 'nearer and more powerful, than the words, or outward relations concerning those things in the Scriptures'. As Penington noted:

> The Lord, in the gospel state, hath promised to be present with his people; not as a wayfaring man, for a night, but to *dwell in them and walk in them*. Yea, if they be tempted and in danger of erring, they shall hear a voice behind them, saying, 'This is the way, walk in it.' Will they not grant this to be a rule, as well as the Scriptures? Nay, is not this a more full direction to the heart, in that state, than it can pick to itself out of the Scriptures? ... the Spirit, which gave forth the words, is greater than the words; therefore we cannot but prize Him himself, and set Him higher in our heart and thoughts, than the words which testify of Him, though they also are very sweet and precious to our taste.[16]

Penington affirms that the Quakers esteemed the Scriptures as 'sweet and precious', but he was equally adamant that the indwelling Spirit was to be regarded as the supreme authority when it came to direction for Christian living and thinking.[17]

In response to this threat to scriptural authority and a Bible-centred spirituality, the Puritans argued that the nature of the Spirit's work in the authors of Scripture was unique and definitely a thing of the past. The Spirit was now *illuminating* that which he had inspired and their experiences of the Spirit were to be tried by the Scriptures. As Richard Baxter (1615-1691), the most prolific of Puritan authors, declared:

> We must not try the Scriptures by our most spiritual apprehensions, but our apprehensions by the Scriptures: that is, we must prefer the Spirit's inspiring the apostles to indite the Scriptures before the Spirit's illuminating of us to understand them, or before any present inspirations, the former being the more perfect; because Christ gave the Apostles the Spirit to deliver us infallibly his own commands, and to indite a

rule for following ages: but he giveth us the Spirit but to understand and use that rule aright. This trying the Spirit by the Scriptures is not a setting of the Scriptures above the Spirit itself; but it is only a trying of the Spirit by the Spirit; that is, the Spirit's operations in themselves and his revelations to any pretenders now, by the Spirit's operations in the Apostles and by their revelations recorded for our use.[18]

From the Puritan point of view, the Quakers made an unbiblical cleavage between the Spirit and the Word. As another Puritan, the London Baptist Benjamin Keach (1640-1704) pointed out: 'Many are confident they have the Spirit, Light, and Power, when 'tis all meer Delusion. The Spirit always leads and directs according to the written Word: "He shall bring my Word", saith Christ, "to your remembrance" [see John 14:26].'[19]

Lest it be thought that the Puritans, in their desire to safeguard a spirituality of the Word, went to the opposite extreme and depreciated the importance of the work of the Spirit in the Christian life, one needs to note the words of the *Second London Confession* 1.5 (1677/1689) — solidly based upon the *Westminster Confession of Faith* (1646) — where it is stated that 'our full persuasion, and assurance of the infallible truth' of the Scriptures comes neither from 'the testimony of the Church of God' nor from the 'heavenliness of the matter' of the Scriptures, the 'efficacy of [their] Doctrine', and 'the Majesty of [their] Stile'. Rather it is only 'the inward work of the Holy Spirit, bearing witness by and with the Word in our Hearts' that convinces believers that God's Word is indeed what it claims to be.[20]

In this regard, Puritan spirituality is thus a marvellous model for us today — a balanced spirituality of Word and Spirit.[21]

'The gymnasium of the soul'

CHAPTER SIX

Prayer and the
CHRISTIAN LIFE

One of the most fragrant names in the Reformed tradition is that of the Scottish Free Church minister of the last century, Andrew Alexander Bonar (1810-1892).[1] A tireless evangelist and champion of heart religion, he is especially remembered today for his biography of his close friend Robert Murray M'Cheyne (1813-1843) and for the published version of his own diary, both of which have become spiritual classics. It has been said that his diary reads like a 'treatise on private prayer'. For example, on the day of his induction into the pastoral charge of Finnieston Free Church, Glasgow, when he was forty-six, he noted in his diary that the Lord had made him feel afresh that 'I must be as much with Him alone as with souls in public'. A few months after this entry he wrote these words regarding the importance of prayer:

> …for nearly ten days past have been much hindered in prayer, and feel my strength weakened thereby. I must at once return,

through the Lord's strength, to not less than *three* hours a day spent in prayer and meditation upon the Word.[2]

While we are certainly not bound by the details of another's practice, yet this diary entry regarding the vital importance of time for prayer surely reveals the high priority that Bonar placed upon this aspect of the Christian life, a priority that he had undoubtedly learned from the Word of God.

When the apostles, for example, delineate in Acts 6:4 what needed to be a priority in their lives, they mention two things in particular, prayer and the ministry of the Word, and it is surely significant that prayer is mentioned first. Likewise, when the apostle Paul comes to conclude his remarks about his future plans in Romans 15 and he asks his readers in Rome to pray for him specifically with regard to some aspects of what he has just told them, he introduces his request with an especially weighty statement.

I appeal to you, brothers, by our Lord Jesus Christ and by the love of the Spirit, to strive together with me in your prayers to God on my behalf, that I may be delivered from the unbelievers in Judea, and that my service for Jerusalem may be acceptable to the saints, so that by God's will I may come to you with joy and be refreshed in your company (Rom. 15:30-32).

The importance that the apostle places on prayer is found in the solemn way that he introduces this passage. He uses the word *parakalō*, translated here by the ESV as 'appeal', but which can also be rendered 'beseech' or 'beg'. The same word is found in Romans 12:1, where it is central to that impressive introduction to the entire section on Christian living (Rom. 12-15:13): 'I appeal to you therefore, brothers, by the mercies of God, to present your bodies as a living sacrifice.' Paul's repetition of this term in Romans 15:30 indicates something of the priority that he wanted his readers to put on prayer.[3] Just as he had appealed to these same readers to present themselves and the entirety of their lives as living sacrifices of worship, so now he urges them to engage meaningfully and regularly in prayer for his ministry.[4] Without such prayer, he intimates, he will be utterly frustrated in his desire to serve God and ultimately fruitless in his service.[5] As the Elizabethan Puritan Richard Greenham noted, in the Christian life 'the Holy Ghost teacheth us that all is nothing without prayer'.[6]

As we look closely at the various elements of this call to prayer, we must note three things in particular:

- First of all, the basis upon which Paul appeals for his readers to pray for him is 'the Lord Jesus Christ' and 'the love of the Spirit';
- Second, there is the nature of prayer — it is nothing less than an arduous, strenuous struggle;
- Third, there are the specific needs for which Paul is requesting prayer, needs that centre on his ministry in Jerusalem and his eventual coming to Rome.

'BY OUR LORD JESUS CHRIST'

Adding to the solemnity of this appeal for prayer is the twofold basis upon which the apostle makes his request. First, the admonition that Paul gives to his readers is 'by our Lord Jesus Christ'. Here Paul invokes the authority of the one Lord, to whom both he and his readers are bound as servants.[7] He says in effect that because Christ is their Lord, they ought to pray for his servant who is seeking the advance of his Master's kingdom and the exaltation of his dear name.

Paul appears to assume two things here. First, if a person is a professing Christian, Paul reckons that he or she is a person who prays. For Paul, to claim that Christ is one's Lord necessarily involves a commitment to prayer. As Richard Baxter expressed it, 'prayer is the breath of the new creature'.[8] And as Baxter's contemporary, Thomas Goodwin (1600-1680), put it, 'our speaking to God by prayers, and his speaking to us by answers thereunto, is one great part of our walking with God'.[9]

When Andrew Fuller (1754-1815), an influential Baptist theologian in the late eighteenth century, came to describe his early religious experience and his conversion, he noted that in the couple of years prior to his actual conversion he had had a number of deeply emotional, religious experiences. These experiences were accompanied by copious tears but, over time, issued in no substantial change of lifestyle. Fuller, for instance, noted after one of them that he 'lived entirely without prayer and was wedded to my sins just the same as before'. After another experience he admitted that he 'continued in the neglect of prayer' and rightfully concluded that whatever profession he may have made at that time, it cannot have been genuine, for to be a Christian is to pray.[10]

Second, Paul assumes that true Christian prayer is first and foremost concerned with the glorification of the triune God and the advance of his kingdom. When the Lord Jesus, for instance, gives to his disciples some broad guidelines as to what the content of their prayer should be, he mentions first of all the exaltation of God and then immediately afterward the advance of his rule in the world: 'Our Father in heaven, hallowed be your name. Your Kingdom come, your will be done on earth as it is in heaven' (Matt. 6:9-10). To be under the authority of Christ is thus to pray specifically for the advance of the gospel and the triumph of Christ.

So, when Paul urges his fellow believers in Rome 'by the Lord Jesus Christ' to pray, he is reminding them of their status. They are numbered among the servants of Christ and as such should be men and women given to prayer that specifically seeks the advance of Christ's cause.

Thus, some questions present themselves:

- Do you profess Christ as your Lord?
- If so, do you pray?
- Do you pray regularly?
- Is prayer a priority in your life?
- What kind of prayers dominate your praying? Prayers for

the advance of the kingdom, or prayers that relate solely to your personal needs and wants?

May God give us a heart and a will to make prayer, prayer for the exaltation of God and the extension of the kingdom, a daily reality in our lives.

'BY THE LOVE OF THE SPIRIT'

Then, Paul also urges them 'by the love of the Spirit' to pray. This is a unique phrase in the Scriptures. Elsewhere when the Scriptures speak of the love of one of the divine persons, it is the love of the Father or the love of Christ.[11] Moreover, it is not immediately clear what Paul means by the phrase. Is it the love that believers have for the Holy Spirit? Or is it the love that the Spirit has for believers? Or should it be understood to mean the love that the Holy Spirit produces in believers for one another?

Few commentators think that the first option is a possibility here. The second has been held by, among others, John Murray, the Presbyterian theologian who taught at Westminster Theological Seminary for much of his life and who wrote a superb commentary on Romans.[12] The interpretation of John Calvin, though, is the one that probably makes the best sense here. He interprets the phrase as the love 'by which the saints ought to embrace one another'.[13]

In this interpretation of the phrase, Paul is basing his appeal on the fact that his readers are indwelt by the Spirit and as such they know something of the love that the Spirit produces in believers for one another. Therefore Paul expects that love for God's people will be demonstrated, in part, by prayer for them. To paraphrase the apostle John: the one who says he loves God's people and never prays for them is a liar.

'PRAYER IS THE GYMNASIUM OF THE SOUL'[14]

Now, prayer is one of the most difficult aspects of the Christian life. We get a glimpse of Paul's recognition of this fact when he goes on to ask the Roman Christians to 'strive together with me in prayers to God for me'. True intercessory prayer, Paul declares, involves strain and arduous struggle, the commitment of energy and earnestness. The word underlying the phrase 'strive together with me' only occurs here in the New Testament, though the similar idea is found in Colossians 2:1-3 and 4:12.

But what is the struggle with? Well, first of all, it is a struggle with the enemy of our souls, Satan, and his demonic hordes. Paul puts it this way in Ephesians 6:12: 'We do not wrestle against flesh and blood, but against the rulers, against the authorities, against the cosmic powers over this present darkness, against the spiritual forces of evil in the heavenly places.' Satan hates God's people at prayer, for he knows that faithful, persevering prayer is a powerful weapon in the hands of the almighty God. As William Cowper (1731-1800), the eighteenth-century poet and hymnwriter, wrote:

> Restraining pray'r, we cease to fight;
>   Pray'r makes the Christian's armour bright;
> And Satan trembles, when he sees
>   The weakest saint upon his knees.[15]

But there is also the struggle against the old nature. Listen to the Puritan preacher John Bunyan (1628-1688) as he describes his own struggle in prayer:

May I but speak my own Experience, and from that tell you the difficulty of Praying to God as I ought; it is enough to make your poor, blind, carnal men, to entertain strange thoughts of me. For, as for my heart, when I go to pray, I find it so loth to go to God, and when it is with him, so loth to stay with him, that many times I am forced in my Prayers; *first* to beg God that he would take mine heart, and set it on himself in Christ, and when it is there, that he would keep it there (Psalm 86.11). Nay, many times I know not what to pray for, I am so blind, nor how to pray I am so ignorant; only (blessed be Grace) the *Spirit helps our infirmities*.

Oh the starting-holes that the heart hath in time of Prayer! none knows how many by-wayes the heart hath, and back-lains, to slip away from the presence of God.[16]

This passage illustrates a few of the most attractive features of Puritan writers like Bunyan: their transparency and their in-depth knowledge of the human heart. From personal experience Bunyan knew the allergic reaction of the sinful nature to the presence of God that still resides in the bosom of every believer. Instead of coming into God's radiant presence to pray, it wants to run and hide — like Adam after he had sinned in the garden. In other words, prayer demands discipline and hard work.

Thus, prayer is a struggle. But Paul expects believers to perse-vere in prayer and know something of the victory of persevering, faithful prayer. Why does he expect this? Because Christians are indwelt by the Spirit of Christ. He has already used this fact as part of his appeal to the Roman Christians to engage in prayer on his behalf. And if he were pressed to give a reason as to why he expects Christians to know a good measure of victory and consistency in prayer, the Spirit and the Spirit's power would surely figure largely in his answer. Were it not for the Spirit, none would be able to persevere in prayer. 'A man without the help of the Spirit', John Bunyan once declared, 'cannot so much as pray once; much less, continue…in a sweet praying frame.'[17]

It needs to be noted that, for all who persevere in this struggle and discipline of prayer, there are times of exquisite delight when the struggle, and duty slides over into pure joy. John Owen, one of John Bunyan's good friends, once observed with regard to Ephesians 2:18 ('Through Christ we have access by one Spirit unto the Father'):

No tongue can express, no mind can reach, the heavenly placidness and soul-satisfying delight which are intimated in these words. To come to God as a Father, through Christ, by the help and assistance of the Holy Spirit, revealing him as a Father unto us, and enabling us to go to him as a Father, how full of sweetness and satisfaction is it![18]

CERTAIN SPECIFIC REQUESTS FOR PRAYER

Paul has three things that he wants the Romans to pray for on his behalf. First, that he might be kept safe from those fanatical Jews in Judea who hated the gospel and who would dearly love to see the apostle of Christ dead. This request in Romans 15:31 indicates that Paul expected his time in Jerusalem to be fraught with tension and danger. While he was thoroughly convinced that it was God's will for him to go up to Jerusalem and fully acquainted with the dangers of going there (Acts 20:22-24), he was by no means reckless and eager to throw his life away. Thus, he asked his brothers and sisters to seek his protection through prayer.

Then, Paul wanted the believers in Rome to pray that the collection of money that he had gathered from the Gentile churches for the 'saints in Jerusalem' (Rom. 15:26-27) would be well received by the Jerusalem church. This was a collection that he had been working on for a number of years (see 1 Cor. 16:1-4; 2 Cor. 8-9), and for Paul it had come to be a concrete display of the unity of Jew and Gentile in Christ.

Finally, there was the desire that he might eventually come to Rome and find rest and refreshment among them. What Paul is thinking of here is spiritual refreshment found in the context of fellowship and preparation for further ministry (see Rom. 15:24,28). This third prayer request is the reason for the first two requests. In other words, what drives the first two requests is the hunger to further extend the reach of the gospel.

AN EARLIER PRAYER REQUEST

Now, five or so years before, Paul had made a similar request of believers in Thessalonica. Writing from the city of Corinth he had asked the Thessalonian Christians to 'pray for us, that the word of the Lord may speed ahead and be honoured, as happened among you, and that we may be delivered from wicked and evil men. For not all have faith' (2 Thess. 3:1-2). And as these Thessalonian believers had prayed, God had moved in the city of Corinth, bringing revival, protecting Paul from the Jewish leaders there who wanted him expelled from the city, and even causing a Roman governor, Gallio (died A.D. 65), to unwittingly befriend the church in that city (see Acts 18:12-16).[19]

This time, though, things turned out quite differently. Paul was nearly killed in a riot in the temple. He ended up a prisoner of the Roman state. He languished in a prison in Palestine for nearly two years. This was followed by a perilous voyage to Rome and a further two-year period of imprisonment in the Roman capital (Acts 21-28).

Would he have concluded that God did not answer his people's prayers? No, not at all. Notice in Romans 15:32 those tremendously important words: 'by the will of God'. Prayer, as the apostle Paul thinks of it, indeed as the Scriptures depict it, is never a presumptuous demanding of God. It is always done in the recognition that God answers his people's prayers in his own ways and in his own time.

Mature spiritual prayers never leave God's sovereignty out of the picture. This deep sense of God's sovereign control over the events of his life does not issue in an attitude of fatalism, in which prayer is regarded as next to useless. On the contrary, Paul knows that God's sovereign purposes are regularly accomplished through the prayers of his people. Thomas Blundel (c.1752-1824), an English Baptist and friend of William Carey, clearly expresses Paul's conviction when he stated that 'it is chiefly in answer to prayer that God has carried on his cause in the world: he could work without any such means; but he does not, neither will he'.[20]

'A great heart warmer'

CHAPTER SEVEN

Christian
MEDITATION

Numerous Bible scholars have noted the parallel between Ephesians 5:18-21 and Colossians 3:16-17. In the former it is being
'filled with the Spirit' that produces such effects as sung worship
that edifies the body of Christ, thanksgiving in all situations, and
mutual submission in the body of Christ. In the latter a similar
list of effects is attributed to the rich indwelling of 'the word
of Christ'. What is the connection between these two? Well,
certainly it would seem that the Spirit fills believers and rules in
their lives when the Word indwells them richly.[1] Listen to these
words of Eugene Peterson:

> The Christian Scriptures are the primary text for Christian
> spirituality. We don't form our personal spiritual lives out of
> a random assemblage of favourite texts in combination with
> individual circumstances; we are formed by the Holy Spirit
> following the text of the Holy Scriptures. God does not put

us in charge of forming our personal spiritualities; we grow in accordance with the revealed Word implanted in us by the [Living]Word.[2]

And to grow in this way we need, among other things, to meditate on the Word.

We probably associate meditation more readily with the practice of the eastern religions than with Christianity, but there is such a thing as Christian and Bible-based meditation.[3]

WHAT IS MEDITATION?

Meditation is clearly not the same as study. It is often a dwelling upon and a 'chewing over' what one has found through hard study of the Scriptures. The nineteenth-century Southern Presbyterian theologian Robert L. Dabney (1820-1898) says of meditation that it is not 'the mental bustle of investigation, but the dwelling of the thought' upon God and his perfections.[4] Meditation most definitely involves thought, for it is not an irrational emptying of our minds as in eastern concepts of meditation. But it involves more than the mind. Its design is 'the raising of the heart to holy affections'.[5]

There is, however, a major problem for Christians in the West with regard to meditation. Our entire system of education 'has trained us almost solely to read for information and skills acquisition'.[6] We thus need to re-form our habit of reading so that we know how to read slowly, savouring every word, mulling it over. The Protestant martyr Thomas Cranmer (1489-1556) puts it well when, in his Collect for the Second Sunday in Advent, he ask for God's grace to 'inwardly digest' the Scriptures:

Blessed Lord, which hast caused all holy Scriptures to be written for our learning; grant us that we may in such wise hear them, read, mark, learn, and inwardly digest them; that by patience and comfort of thy holy word, we may embrace, and ever hold fast the blessed hope of everlasting life, which thou hast given us in our saviour Jesus Christ.[7]

SUBJECTS FOR MEDITATION

The Scriptures offer to us a variety of themes for meditation.

- God's law and decrees (Josh. 1:8; Ps. 119:23,97)
- God's works (Ps. 77:12; Luke 2:19,51[8])
- What is just and true (Phil. 4:8)
- God's Word (Ps. 1:1-2)
- God's splendour and majesty (Ps. 145:5)
- God's wonders (Ps. 119:27)

Probably what is most obvious about this list is the 'weightiness' of the subjects. While all Scripture is given us by God for edification, for our hearts to be warmed and our wills strengthened in meditation we must mull over and meditate upon 'the infinities and immensities' of God's words and deeds. Thus, Nathanael Ranew, a leading Puritan in the county of Essex who was once described as 'a judicious divine, generally esteemed and valued', says we should meditate on such things as:[9]

- the 'infinitely glorious and all-sufficient God, the Father, Son, and Holy Spirit'
- God's creation — its vastness and the diversity of creatures within it
- God's sovereign rule over creation and his providential working among angels and men
- the fall of some angels and all of humanity
- the redemption of some men and women by Christ the Redeemer and their eternal salvation
- death and the final judgement, heaven and hell
- the ordinances of Christ and the covenant of grace
- our own spiritual estate

From this list it is clear that the power and blessing of meditation does not lie in the technique but in the *content*, the truth itself.

THE WAY OF MEDITATING

A number of hints are given in Scripture to help us in the actual practice of meditation.

First, we need to be in a place of quiet of solitude. Isaac went out to a field to meditate (Gen. 24:63) and David meditated alone on his bed (Ps. 63:6).

Then, it is vital to approach meditation in the right frame of mind. What are we doing in meditation? We are seeking the living God. We desire to hear his voice in the Word and do his will.[10]

Third, we need to have a plan for consistently reading Scripture. What is important here is ongoing engagement with the text of Scripture.

Fourth, memorization of Scripture can be a great help. Memorization of Scripture plants Scripture deep within the soul from whence it can begin to re-shape the human life.

As one first begins to meditate, it can be helpful to read aloud the passage that is the subject of meditation and then re-read it as one goes on.

Sixth, to meditate profitably requires time. This is a challenge in our busy world. If one asks how much time, the Puritan Thomas Watson (died c.1690) answers, 'If when a man is cold you ask how long he should stand by the fire? Sure, till he be thoroughly warm, and made fit for his work.'[11] This need for taking time in this great task of the soul is found in the following remarks by Ranew:

> Meditation is not a hasty hurry of thoughts... It is not gathering half-ripe fruit... We will not have (for want of time) our...meat raw-roasted; knowing that what is not rightly prepared for the body, may breed distempers, if it bring not death. ...[So] why should we gather our soul's precious fruits half-ripe?[12]

Carving out great chunks of time is not the only way to meditate, however. The psalmist speaks often of how he meditated 'day and night' (Ps. 1:2) by which he presumably does not mean that he did nothing but meditate all day! No, he means that he had cultivated the ability to turn his thoughts naturally to spiritual matters even as he engaged in his daily tasks and responsibilities.

Seventh, we can use a hymnbook to guide us and stir us up to heavenly themes. It would take us too far afield to write about the folly of the current worship trend in throwing away our hymnals in favour of overheads, but here is one vital reason to save our hymnals.

Eighth, we need to learn to ask questions of the text that has been chosen for meditation. Edmund Clowney (1917-2005), for example, has a stimulating question for meditation in connection with John 3:16: 'Why does John 3:16 not read, "For God so loved his only Son that he gave him the world"?' Interrogating the text helps us to chew over its content and draw out the quintessence of its life-giving vitamins.

And, finally, meditation should issue in prayer as we respond to what we hear God saying in the text of the Word.

THE GOAL OF MEDITATION

The psalms in particular give us some indication of the effects and benefits that meditation brings. In the first instance, and in accord with the psalms' emphasis on the heart, meditation is done with a view to rousing such affections as desire, love and delight. As Nathanael Ranew says, 'Right and genuine meditation is an affectionate thing; as the head acts, the heart glows.'[13] And again he remarks: 'Meditation is that which keeps alive the fire on the altar, and helps to make it burn… Meditation is a great heart warmer…'[14]

So also David testified that through his meditations, his heart 'became hot within' him and as he meditated 'the fire burned' (Ps. 39:3). Meditation and affection are thus closely linked. But if the affections have been rightly roused, they should constrain the will to action. David's 'hot heart' bubbled over into a zeal for prayer: 'then I spoke with my tongue: "O Lord, make me know my end…"' (Ps. 39:3-4). And so meditation and prayer are joined together.

Then, the great psalm with which the Book of Psalms begins, Psalm 1, emphasizes the purpose of meditation as being a means to obedience. It is the man who 'meditates day and night' upon the law of God, delighting in it, who will find himself preserved from walking in 'the counsel of the wicked' and from standing in 'the way of sinners' and from sitting in 'the seat of scoffers'.[15] It appears then, that meditation and piety go hand in hand.

Meditation is thus key to fostering what Reformed authors and preachers have long designated as 'heart religion'. It is by means of this sort of biblical meditation that Christians enter into true delight and joy (Ps. 1:2; 104:34) and spiritual wisdom and under-standing (Ps. 49:3; 119:97-98). Well did Thomas Watson write: 'It gives us a true account why there are so few good Christians in the world; namely because there are so few meditating Christians... so much of the vitals and spirit of religion lies in it.'[16]

JONATHAN EDWARDS — A MODEL OF MEDITATION

A fabulous model of biblical meditation is the eighteenth-cen-tury American theologian, Jonathan Edwards. Like Tyndale and the Puritans referred to previously,[17] he was convinced that the Scriptures 'are the light by which ministers must be enlightened, and the light they are to hold forth to their hearers; and they are the fire whence their hearts and the hearts of their hearers must be enkindled'.[18] Not surprisingly, biblical meditation was central to his piety. Samuel Hopkins (1721-1803), one of his close friends and his first biographer, noted that Edwards was, 'as far as it can be known, much on his knees in secret, and in devout reading of God's word and meditation upon it'.[19]

Not long after his conversion Edwards drew up what are known as his *Resolutions* (1722-1723) in which, at the outset of his minis-try, he committed himself to keeping a list of 70 guidelines to help him stay passionate in his pursuit of God and his glory.[20] Hopkins commented that these *Resolutions* 'may justly be considered as the foundation and plan of his whole life'.[21] Though comparatively young when he wrote them, they reflect a mature understanding of genuine spirituality and the way such spirituality should be evident in all of one's life and pursued with ardour and zeal. There is one resolution that deals especially with the Scriptures. 'Resolution 28' stated what Edwards hoped would be a lifelong characteristic of the way he approached Scripture. He declared that he was '[r]esolved, to study the Scriptures so steadily, constantly, and frequently, as that I may find, and plainly perceive, myself to grow in the knowledge of the same'.[22] The adverbs Edwards uses here — 'steadily, constantly, and frequently' — surely indicate his desire to continually saturate his mind with Scripture.

A full twenty-two years later, while preaching at the ordination of a certain Robert Abercrombie (d.1780) on 30 August 1744, he uttered the exact same sentiments, though in different words. Ministers of the gospel, Edwards argued, 'should be very conversant with the Holy Scriptures; making it very much their business, with the utmost diligence and strictness, to search these holy writings'.[23] The phrase 'with the utmost diligence and strictness' makes the same point as 'steadily, constantly, and frequently' in 'Resolution 28'. What Edwards appears to be encouraging in both of these texts is nothing less than saturating the heart and mind with Scriptural truth and the meta-narrative of the Bible, something accomplished by the practice of biblical meditation. This can be readily seen from a third text in which he describes his encounter with Scripture after his conversion. This text also makes it abundantly clear that he is not merely thinking of academic Bible study in the passages we have cited.

I had then, and at other times, the greatest delight in the holy Scriptures, of any book whatsoever. Oftentimes in reading it, every word seemed to touch my heart. I felt an harmony between something in my heart, and those sweet and powerful words. I seemed often to see so much light, exhibited by every sentence, and such a refreshing ravishing food communicated, that I could not get along in reading. Used oftentimes to dwell long on one sentence, to see the wonders contained in it; and yet almost every sentence seemed to be full of wonders.[24]

This pattern of meditation upon God's holy Word, one that was part of Edwards' Puritan heritage, appears to have been central to Edwards' walk with God in the later years of his life as well. Samuel Hopkins noted that Edwards 'had an uncommon thirst for knowledge, in the pursuit of which, he spared no cost nor pains'. He thus 'read all the books, especially books of divinity', that he could get hold of. But, Hopkins emphasized, 'he studied the Bible more than all other books, and more than most other divines do. His uncommon acquaintance with the Bible appears in his sermons, and in most of his publications; and his great pains in studying it are manifest in his manuscript notes upon it.'[25]

A good example of the fruit of his lifelong meditation on Scripture can be seen in what has been termed Edwards' 'Blank Bible'. This was a small printed Bible that Edwards owned in which blank sheets were placed between all of the pages. These blank sheets were divided into two columns so that Edwards could then write commentary on adjacent texts. Edwards' 'Blank Bible' contains as many as 10,000 entries, written on the entire Bible between 1730 and 1758.[26]

May God enable us who are evangelicals — and who claim to prize the Scriptures in our day as Edwards treasured them in his — to be as assiduous in spiritual meditation as our renowned forebear!

'Guardians of the soul'

CHAPTER EIGHT

Spiritual friendship
AS A MEANS OF GRACE [1]

Our culture is not one that provides great encouragement for the nurture and development of deep, long-lasting, satisfying friendships. Such friendships take time and sacrifice, and western culture in the early twenty-first century is a busy, busy world that as a rule is far more interested in receiving and possessing than in sacrificing and giving. And where such friendships are found, it is usually among women. Friendships among men in our culture are often superficial, rarely deep or close.[2]

What is especially disturbing about this fact is that western Christianity is little different from its culture. The English Anglican writer C. S. Lewis (1898-1963) has an ingenious little book entitled *The Screwtape Letters*, a remarkable commentary on spiritual warfare from the point of view of our enemy. In it there is one letter from the senior devil, Screwtape, to his nephew Wormwood in which Screwtape rejoices over the fact that 'in modern Christian writings' there is to be found 'few of the old warnings about Worldly Vanities, the Choice of Friends, and the Value of Time'.[3] Now, whether or not Lewis is right with regard to a scarcity of twentieth-century Christian literature about 'Worldly Vanities' and 'the Value of Time', he is undoubtedly correct when it comes to the topic of friendship.

How different in this respect is our world from that of the ancients, both pagan and Christian. In the ancient world friendship was deemed to be of such vital importance that the pagan philosopher Plato (428-348 B.C.) devoted an entire book, the *Lysis*, as well as substantial portions of two other books, the *Phaedrus* and the *Symposium*, to a treatment of its nature. Aristotle (384-322 B.C.), the other leading thinker of the classical Greek period, also considered the topic of friendship significant enough to have a discussion of it occupy two of the ten books of the *Nicomachean Ethics*, his major work on ethical issues. For the ancient Greeks — and this is true also of the Romans — friendship formed one of the highest ideals of human life.

THE SCRIPTURES ON FRIENDSHIP

While we do not find such extended discussions of the concept of friendship in the Scriptures, we do come across reflections on friendship like the passage in Ecclesiastes 4:9-12:

> Two are better than one, because they have a good reward for their toil. For if they fall, one will lift up his fellow. But woe to him who is alone when he falls and has not another to lift him up! Again, if two lie together, they keep warm, but how can one keep warm alone? And though a man might prevail against one who is alone, two will withstand him — a threefold cord is not quickly broken.

There are also marvellous illustrations of what friendship should be like, e.g. the friendship of Ruth and Naomi, or that of David and Jonathan. Then there are the nuggets of advice about having friends and keeping them in that Old Testament compendium of wisdom, Proverbs.[4] Reading through such texts as these, one comes away with the impression that the world of the Bible regards friendship as a very important part of life.

Now, the Bible uses two consistent images in its representation of friendship.[5] The first is that of *the knitting of souls together.* Deuteronomy provides the earliest mention in this regard when it speaks of a 'friend who is as your own soul' (Deut. 13:6), that is, one who is a companion of one's innermost thoughts and feelings. Prominent in this reflection on friendship is the concept of intimacy. It is well illustrated by Jonathan and David's friendship. For example, in 1 Samuel 18:1 we read that the 'soul of Jonathan was knit to the soul of David, and Jonathan loved him as his own soul'.[6] This reflection on the meaning of friendship bears with it ideas of strong emotional attachment and loyalty.[7] Not surprisingly, the term 'friend' naturally became another name for believers or brothers and sisters in the Lord (see 3 John 14).

The second image that the Bible uses to represent friendship is *the face-to-face encounter.* This is literally the image used for Moses' relationship to God. In the tabernacle God spoke to Moses 'face to face, as a man speaks to his friend' (Exod. 33:11; see also Num. 12:8). The face-to-face image implies a conversation, a sharing of confidences and consequently a meeting of minds, goals and direction. In the New Testament, we find a similar idea expressed in 2 John 12, where the Elder tells his readers that he wants to speak to them 'face to face'. One of the benefits of such face-to-face encounters between friends is the heightened insight that such times of friendship produce. As the famous saying in Proverbs 27:17 puts it, 'Iron sharpens iron, and one man sharpens another.'

PAUL AND TIMOTHY

In the New Testament, one finds a powerful witness to the fact that Christian friendship and fellowship are one of the great sources of spiritual strength in the letters of the apostle Paul. The more you read Paul's letters the more you realize that Paul is rarely to be found without co-workers, friends and acquaintances.

Samuel Johnson (1709-1784), the eighteenth-century author and lexicographer, once said about his friend Sir John Hawkins that he was 'a most unclubbable man'. Such a remark could not be said of Paul. He was very 'clubbable', a gregarious man who 'delighted in the company of his fellows'.[8] And of his companions the dearest would have to have been Timothy. Though he was probably twenty years or so Paul's junior, Timothy became the apostle's closest friend. In the words of F. F. Bruce (1910-1990), Timothy 'readily surrendered whatever personal ambitions he might have cherished in order to play the part of a son to Paul and help him in his missionary activity, showing a selfless concern for others that matched the apostle's own eagerness to spend and be spent for them'.[9]

Timothy had joined the apostle Paul's ministry team early on in what is termed Paul's second missionary journey, that is, around A.D. 48 or 49 (see Acts 16:1-13). As he travelled with Paul he saw first-hand Paul's 'doctrine, manner of life, purpose, faith, long-suffering, love, perseverance, persecutions, afflictions' (2 Tim. 3:10-11). As the two men spent this large amount of time together Timothy's soul began to mirror that of Paul, and his mind became increasingly attuned to the wavelengths of the apostle's thinking. Thus, Timothy's friendship with Paul was a means by which God sanctified the younger man, giving him an ever-increasing rich-ness of thought about God and the gospel, and an ever-growing desire for holiness and conformity to Christ.

In 1 Corinthians 15:33 Paul urges the Corinthians to recognize that 'evil company corrupts good habits'. Intimate friendships with evil characters will invariably have a negative effect on our lives. Likewise, one can say that 'good company promotes good habits'. This was the effect that Paul undoubtedly had on Timothy. This was the effect that friendship with the eighteenth-century Baptist Samuel Pearce (1766-1799), a man of great personal holiness, had on the Congregationalist William Jay (1769-1853). Jay, who had an influential ministry in Bath, England, for the first half of the nineteenth century, had this comment about the last time that he saw Pearce alive: 'What a savour does communion with such a man leave upon the spirit.'[10] In the words of Maurice Roberts: 'Our best friends are those whose company most makes us afraid to sin.'[11]

Probably the clearest text in which the dearness of Paul's friendship with Timothy comes out is Philippians 2:19-22. The Philippian church had been evidently experiencing some measure of disunity. Paul mentions it explicitly in chapter 4 when he urges Euodia and Syntyche 'to agree (*to auto phronein*) in the Lord' (verse 2). In chapter 2 Paul devotes a lengthy section of this letter to resolving this problem. He begins by urging the Philippians to be 'of the same mind' (*to auto phronēte*) — essentially the same phrase that Paul employs in Philippians 4:2 — 'having the same love, being in full accord and of one mind', looking out for not only their own interests but also those of others (Phil. 2:2-4).

To illustrate this admonition and drive it home Paul encourages the Philippians to meditate on the example of Christ, whose mind and heart were focused not on his own personal interests but on those of fallen humanity. So taken up was Christ with the lot of sinners that though he was fully God he 'made himself nothing'. He became incarnate, and willingly and humbly he took upon himself the burden of human sin and was 'obedient to the point of death, even death on a cross' (Phil. 2:7-8).

The apostle, though, does not leave this theme of thinking of others' best interests after he has outlined the work of Christ. In Philippians 2:19-22 he gives a second example of being like-minded and having the interests of others at heart. This time he turns to his friend Timothy.

> I hope in the Lord Jesus to send Timothy to you soon, so that I too may be cheered by news of you. For I have no one like him, who will be genuinely concerned for your welfare. They all seek their own interests, not those of Jesus Christ. But you know Timothy's proven worth, how as a son with a father he has served with me in the gospel.

From the words and phrases that Paul uses here it is clear that he is recommending Timothy as an example of Christ-likeness. Unlike others that Paul knows, Timothy sincerely cares for the state of the Philippians. He is genuinely concerned about the needs of other believers and is not solely seeking to promote his own interests. And as such he displays the mind of Christ. Paul can thus describe him in verse 20 as being likeminded to Paul: because of his desire to be like Christ, Timothy is one who fully shares Paul's heart and mind and is thus a completely trustworthy companion and friend of Paul.

Due to their age difference, Paul naturally speaks of Timothy as his son. He goes on to say that Timothy has proven his worth during his ministry with Paul 'as a son with his father'. But he quickly adds that Timothy has not been serving him but the gospel. Paul is always very careful to avoid giving the impression that he is lord and master over the faith of others. Timothy did not serve him, but together, as equals before God, they served the Lord of the gospel, Christ.

In this text from Philippians we see clearly the way that Paul prizes his friendship with Timothy and the way that it is based on a harmony of heart and mind. Without such harmony there can be no intimate friendship.

AN OVERVIEW OF FRIENDSHIP IN THE CHRISTIAN TRADITION

It is instructive to observe that the spread of the church throughout the Roman Empire in the centuries immediately after the New Testament era did not negate this rich appreciation of friendship. Despite the Christian emphasis on showing love to all men and women — family, friends, acquaintances, even enemies — friendship continued to be highly valued. In fact, the emphasis placed on the unity in Christ of all Christians encouraged a high degree of spiritual intimacy that resembled, and even surpassed, the intimacy considered by Graeco-Roman paganism to be essential to the experience of genuine friendship.[12]

Gregory of Nazianzus (*c.* A.D. 329-389), a leading fourth-century Greek Christian theologian, could thus write of his friendship with Basil of Caesarea (*c.* A.D. 330-379) during their time together as students in Athens in the 350s:

> In studies, in lodgings, in discussions I had him as companion. …We had all things in common… But above all it was God, of course, and a mutual desire for higher things, that drew us to each other. As a result we reached such a pitch of confidence that we revealed the depths of our hearts, becoming ever more united in our yearning.[13]

Given this estimation of friendship, it is no surprise that Gregory could also state: 'If anyone were to ask me, "What is the best thing in life?", I would answer, "Friends".'[14]

At the beginning of the modern era, John Calvin, who has had the undeserved reputation of being cold and harsh and unloving, also had a rich appreciation of friendship. The French Reformed historian Richard Stauffer reckoned that there were few men at the time of the Reformation 'who developed as many friendships' as Calvin.[15] Two of his closest friends were his fellow Reformers William Farel (1489-1565) and Pierre Viret (1511-1571). Calvin celebrated his friendship with these two men in his preface to his *Commentary on Titus*, where he stated:

> I do not believe that there have ever been such friends who have lived together in such a deep friendship in their everyday style of life in this world as we have in our ministry. I have served here in the office of pastor with you two. There was never any appearance of envy; it seems to me that you two and I were as one person. …And we have shown through visible witness and good authority before men that we have among us no other understanding or friendship than that which has been dedicated to the name of Christ, has been to the present time of profit to his church, and has

no other purpose but that all may be one in him with us.[16]

This brotherly friendship is expressed in the correspondence of these three men. There are extant 163 letters from Calvin to Farel, 137 from Farel to Calvin, 204 letters from Calvin to Viret, and 185 from Viret to Calvin. In this invaluable correspondence, not only are theological problems and ecclesiastical matters frankly discussed, but there is also an openness in relation to the problems of their private lives.

To note but one example. On 27 January 1552, Calvin wrote to Farel and chided him for reports that he had heard — true reports one must add — about the undue length of Farel's sermons. 'You have often confessed', Calvin reminds his friend, 'that you know this is a fault and that you would like to correct it.' Calvin went on to encourage Farel to shorten his sermons lest Satan use Farel's failing in this regard to destroy the many good things being produced by his ministry.

TWO BAPTIST FRIENDS

Another excellent illustration of a biblical friendship is that of John Ryland, Jr (1753-1825) and Andrew Fuller. From 1781 to 1793, Ryland was involved in the pastoral leadership of College Lane Baptist Church with his father, John Ryland, Sr (d.1792) in Northampton.[17] Later, in 1793, he was called to be the pastor of Broadmead Baptist Church in Bristol, England, as well as the principal of Bristol Baptist Academy, both positions being held concurrently. He stayed in these offices till his death in 1825. Now, all of the institutions in which Ryland served were part of the Calvinistic Baptist denomination in Great Britain, the largest Baptist group of that era.

Among Ryland's lifelong friends, indeed his closest friend, was Andrew Fuller.[18] Fuller was born in Wicken, a small agricultural village in Cambridgeshire. His parents Robert Fuller (1723-1781) and Philippa Gunton (1726-1816), were farmers who rented a succession of dairy farms. In 1761, his parents moved a short distance to Soham, where he and his family began to regularly attend the local Calvinistic Baptist church, and where Fuller was converted in November 1769. After being baptized the following spring, he became a member of the Soham church. In 1774 Fuller was called to the pastorate of this work. He stayed until 1782, when he became the pastor of the Calvinistic Baptist congregation at Kettering.

His time as a pastor in Soham was a decisive period for the shaping of Fuller's theological perspective. It was during this period that he began a lifelong study of the works of the American divine Jonathan Edwards, which, along with his commitment to live under the authority of the infallible Scriptures, enabled him to become what his close friend John Ryland, Jr described as 'perhaps the most judicious and able theological writer that ever belonged to our denomination'.[19] Succeeding generations have confirmed Ryland's estimation of his friend. C. H. Spurgeon, for instance, once described Fuller as the 'greatest theologian' of his century, while A. C. Underwood, the Baptist historian of this century, said of Fuller — in a statement that clearly echoes Ryland's estimation — that 'he was the soundest and most creatively useful theologian the Particular Baptists have ever had'.[20] David Phillips, a nineteenth-century Welsh biographer, may have put it best when he called Fuller 'the elephant of Kettering', an allusion to his weighty theological influence.[21] He also served as the first Secretary of the Baptist Missionary Society, founded in 1792, from its inception until his death in 1815.

Ryland and Fuller first met in 1778 when both of them were young men and they were wrestling with a number of extremely important theological issues. Within a year they were the closest of friends. After Fuller moved to Kettering in 1782 the two of them had frequent opportunities to talk, to pray and to spend time together, for Northampton and Kettering are only thirteen miles apart. Their friendship was to be unbroken for the next thirty-seven years, till Fuller's death in 1815.

Nine days before he died, Fuller asked one last request of Ryland:

would he preach his funeral sermon?[22] Ryland agreed, though it would have been no easy task for him to hold back his tears as he spoke. Towards the end of this sermon, Ryland reminisced about the fact that their friendship had 'never met with one minute's interruption, by one unkind word or thought, of which I have any knowledge' and that the wound caused by the loss of 'this most faithful and judicious friend' was something that would never be healed in this life.[23]

THE COST OF FRIENDSHIP

The year following Fuller's death, Ryland published a biography of his close friend. In the introduction, he stated the following about their friendship: 'Most of our common acquaintance are well aware, that I was his oldest and most intimate friend; and though my removal to Bristol, above twenty years ago, placed us at a distance from each other, yet a constant correspondence was all along maintained; and, to me at least, it seemed a tedious interval, if more than a fortnight elapsed without my receiving a letter from him.'[24]

When Ryland moved from Northampton to Bristol in 1793 he was no longer close enough to his friend in Kettering for them to meet on a regular basis. The only way that they could keep their friendship alive and intact was through the medium of the letter. Thus, for more than twenty years, they faithfully corresponded with one another, and Ryland notes that if he did not hear from Fuller at least once every two weeks he found it 'tedious', that is, painful and upsetting.[25] Both Ryland and Fuller knew that their friendship was a fragile treasure that could be easily lost or neglected in the busy-ness of life if they did not give it the attention it needed. How true it is that even strong friendships like that of Ryland and Fuller need, to use some words of Haddon Robinson, 'watering, or they shrivel up and blow away'.[26] How many friendships have died simply because we have not put into them the time they needed to flourish.

FRIENDSHIP — WARTS AND ALL

What had initially attracted Ryland and Fuller to one another was the discovery that they shared 'a strong attachment to the same religious principles, a decided aversion to the same errors, a predilection for the same authors', in particular, Jonathan Edwards.[27] In other words, they had that fundamental aspect of a good friendship: a union of hearts. They found deep joy in their oneness of soul — their passion for the glory of Christ and the extension of his kingdom. But friends are not Siamese twins or clones of one another. It belongs to the essence of genuine friendship that friends accept one another for what they are, 'warts and all', and they give one another room to disagree.[28]

In the case of Ryland and Fuller their main difference of opinion revolved around what was an extremely volatile issue among eighteenth-century English-speaking Baptists: the issue of open and closed communion, and open and closed membership. Now, in the eighteenth century the vast majority of pastors and congregations in the Calvinistic Baptist denomination, including Fuller, adhered to a policy of closed membership — that is, only baptized believers could become members of their local churches — and closed communion — that is, only baptized believers could partake of the Lord's Supper in their meeting-houses. Ryland, on the other hand, was of the conviction that both the Lord's Supper and membership in the local church should be open to all Christians, regardless of whether or not they had been baptized as believers. He was thus committed to a policy of both open communion and open membership.

When Ryland was the pastor of the College Lane Church in Northampton, for instance, one of the leading deacons, a certain Thomas Trinder, did not receive believer's baptism until six years after he had been appointed deacon. Fuller would never have tolerated such a situation in the church that he pastored in Kettering. But the two men were secure enough in their friendship to disagree and not have it destroy their friendship.

The only time that this theological difference really came close to disturbing their friendship was in connection with the Baptist Missionary Society's mission at Serampore, India.[29] Headed by William Carey, William Ward (1769-1823) and Joshua Marshman (1768-1837), all of whom were friends of Ryland and Fuller, this mission adopted a policy of open communion in 1805. Writing to Fuller that year, the Serampore missionaries informed him they had come to the conviction that:

> No one has a right to debar a true Christian from the Lord's table, nor refuse to communicate with a real Christian in commemorating the death of their common Lord, without being guilty of a breach of the Law of Love, which law is addressed to us as Christians, and not as Baptists or Paedo-baptists. …We cannot doubt whether a Watts, an Edwards, a Brainerd, a Doddridge, a Whitfield [sic], did right in partaking of the Lord's Supper, though really unbaptized, or whether they had the presence of God at the Lord's table?[30]

Fuller was deeply disturbed by this reasoning and the decision made by the Serampore missionaries and exerted all of his powers of influence and reasoning to convince them to embrace closed communion, which they eventually did in 1811. Ryland, though, was not slow to criticize this reversal of policy. But, as he later said of his disagreement with Fuller: 'I repeatedly expressed myself more freely and strongly to him, than I did to any man in England; yet without giving him offence.'[31]

We are all subject to the temptation to make our views about secondary matters far more important than they actually are and to squeeze our friends into our own mould when it comes to these less than primary issues. Fuller and Ryland, on the other hand, genuinely knew how to give each other space to disagree on what many of their Baptist acquaintances regarded as an all-essential issue. In so doing they revealed that they were seeking to shape their friendship along the lines of that old adage: 'In things essential, unity; in non-essentials, liberty; in all things, charity.'

THE ONE *ESSENTIAL* FRIENDSHIP

When Fuller lay dying in April 1815, he was asked if he wanted to see Ryland, his oldest living friend. His response was terse: 'He can do me no good.' His reply seems to be an odd statement, lacking in appreciation for what their long friendship had meant to the two men. But it needs to be understood in context. In his final letter to Ryland, Fuller had begun by saying: 'We have enjoyed much together, which I hope will prove an earnest of greater enjoyment in another world. ...[There] I trust we shall meet, and part no more.'[32] Clearly, his feelings about his friendship with Ryland had undergone no alteration whatsoever. In the light of his impending death, however, there was only one friendship that he knew to be needful in that moment: his friendship with the triune God — Father, Son and Holy Spirit. As another eighteenth-century writer, an Anglican rector by the name of James Newton, had written when faced with the death of his brother: 'If we have God for our Friend, what need we to fear, Nothing, but without his Friendship we may be looked on as the most miserable of Men.'[33]

*'True churches of Jesus Christ travail in birth
for the salvation of men'*

CHAPTER NINE

Mission – the inevitable
FRUIT OF TRUE SPIRITUALITY

Historically, where there has been spiritual vitality and life in
evangelical circles, there has been a concern for mission, prayerful
and active concern for the salvation of the lost.[1] Reflect on these
three examples — all taken from the Baptist tradition.

First, that quintessential nineteenth-century Baptist, C. H. Spurgeon, who, at the age of twenty-five and not long after he had been
called to be the pastor of the Metropolitan Tabernacle, solemnly
resolved: 'God sparing my life, if I have my people at my back I will
not rest until the dark county of Surrey [which lay to the south of
London, where his church was located] be covered with places of
worship.'[2]

Andrew Fuller, the respected eighteenth-century theologian
and pastor, echoed similar sentiments when he declared that the
'true churches of Jesus Christ travail in birth for the salvation of
men. They are the armies of the Lamb, the grand object of whose
existence is to extend the Redeemer's kingdom'.[3]

Finally, John Bunyan, the seventeenth-century pastor and author of the Christian classic *Pilgrim's Progress*, who was deeply admired by both Spurgeon and Fuller, once said that the 'great desire' of his heart was

> to get into the darkest places in the Countrey, even amongst those people that were furthest off of profession; yet not because I could not endure the light (for I feared not to shew my Gospel to any) but because I found my spirit leaned most after awakening and converting Work, and the Word that I carried did lean itself most that way; Yea, so have I strived to preach the Gospel, not where Christ was named, lest I should build upon another mans foundation, Rom. 15.20. In my preaching I have really been in pain, and have as it were travailed to bring forth Children to God; neither could I be satisfied unless some fruits did appear in my work: if I were fruitless it matter'd not who commended me; but if I were fruitful, I cared not who did condemn.[4]

What helped to fuel these three men's zeal for the salvation of lost men and women was the example of early Christians like the apostle Paul. Bunyan, in fact, explicitly cites a verse in which the apostle's passion for evangelism is most evident — Romans 15:20: 'I make it my ambition to preach the gospel, not where Christ has already been named, lest I build on someone else's foundations.' This verse is part of a somewhat larger passage, Romans 15:18-24, which is found in the midst of Paul's concluding remarks to what is his most systematic exposition of the nature of the gospel as it relates to doctrine and lifestyle. It offers a very important window of understanding into Paul's thinking about his calling as an apostle.

At the very outset of his letter to the Romans Paul had told the believers in Rome of his hopes to come to see them, to encourage them and strengthen them through the preaching of the gospel, and to be encouraged by them in return (1:10-15). At the end of the letter, in Romans 15:14-24, he comes back to these travel plans:

I myself am satisfied about you, my brothers, that you your-
selves are full of goodness, filled with all knowledge and able
to instruct one another. But on some points I have written
to you very boldly by way of reminder, because of the grace
given me by God to be a minister of Christ Jesus to the
Gentiles in the priestly service of the gospel of God, so that
the offering of the Gentiles may be acceptable, sanctified by
the Holy Spirit. In Christ Jesus, then, I have reason to be
proud of my work for God. For I will not venture to speak of
anything except what Christ has accomplished through me
to bring the Gentiles to obedience — by word and deed, by
the power of signs and wonders, by the power of the Spirit
of God — so that from Jerusalem and all the way around
to Illyricum I have fulfilled the ministry of the gospel of
Christ; and thus I make it my ambition to preach the gospel,
not where Christ has already been named, lest I build on
someone else's foundation, but as it is written,

'Those who have never been told of him will see, and
those who have never heard will understand.'

This is the reason why I have so often been hindered from
coming to you. But now, since I no longer have any room for
work in these regions, and since I have longed for many years
to come to you, I hope to see you in passing as I go to Spain,
and to be helped on my journey there by you, once I have
enjoyed your company for a while.

Here, Paul emphasizes four things in particular. First, there is
in verse 15 an overwhelming sense of God's unmerited favour,
his grace and mercy, which lay at the foundation of his entire
ministry to the Gentiles. Then, God's grace at work in the past is
mentioned as Paul tells his readers about the shape of his ministry
up to that point and the main area of the Mediterranean in which
it had been located. Third, Paul speaks of grace at work in the

future as he goes on to inform the Roman believers of his future plans to visit them in Rome and his hope that with their support he will be able to move on from there to the western extremity of the Roman Empire, Spain. Finally, this passage tellingly reveals the heart of the apostle's ministry: the glorification of God in the establishment of local churches.

MISSIONARY LABOURS IN THE EASTERN MEDITERRANEAN

Paul was quite conscious that he was called to be a pioneer evangelist and a builder of foundations. At his commissioning as an apostle, he had been explicitly told by the risen Christ that he was being sent to the Gentiles 'to open their eyes, so that they may turn from darkness to light and from the power of Satan to God' (Acts 26:18). And over the next twenty years Paul unashamedly proclaimed the gospel in such strongholds of Satan as Cyprus and Ephesus, Athens and Corinth. As he preached and taught, the power of the Holy Spirit accompanied his preaching (Rom. 15:19). Numerous Gentiles were drawn by that power out of the darkness of spiritual death and freed from their bondage to sin, brought into the light of God's kingdom and joined to other believers in local churches, delivered from the clutches of Satan and made alive to God.

Paul consciously made it his aim, he tells us in Romans 15:20, to proclaim the gospel in cities and towns where the glorious name of Jesus Christ had never been named in worship, and never acknowledged and confessed as Lord. And by the grace of God churches had been founded in key centres and major cities from Jerusalem all the way to the region of Illyricum, which ran down the eastern coast of the Adriatic Gulf, occupying today what is Albania and what was Yugoslavia (Rom. 15:15,19). Paul's ministry had been focused on the north-eastern quadrant of the Mediterranean. His use in verse 19 of the term *kyklō* — which literally means 'in a circle', that is, 'in a sweep around' — sees the line from Jerusalem to Illyricum as part of a larger circle of mission. Paul was specifically led by the Spirit of God to target this geographical area as the locale of his early ministry.[5]

There is no indication at all in any of Paul's writings or in the Book of Acts that he ever considered exercising a ministry as a church-planter in Egypt or other parts of the southern Mediterranean coast, or towards peoples outside of the Roman Empire, like the Parthians to the east of the Empire or the Germanic tribes to the north.[6] Obviously Paul left it to other pioneer evangelists to take the gospel to these regions. What he knew, though, was that God had called him to evangelize this particular region on the northern coast of the Mediterranean.

It is significant that Paul describes his ministry in verse 20 as one of laying foundations. This was an image that he had also used in 1 Corinthians 3:10 when he thought about the exact shape of his life's work. There he informs his readers that it was as a 'skilled master builder' that he had laid 'the foundation' of the church in Corinth. It is hardly accidental that Paul does not describe the shape of his ministry as one of simply making bricks, that is, the winning of individual Gentiles to Christ. Rather, Paul pictures himself in both of these verses as a builder of 'buildings', that is, a founder of communities that are Christ-centred in their worship, their doctrine, and their life.[7]

His goal as a pioneer evangelist and missionary was not only the saving of the lost, but also the gathering together of those who had been converted into communities of like-minded men and women. New Testament scholar P. T. O'Brien puts it this way: for Paul 'conversion to Christ meant incorporation into him, and thus membership within a Christian community'.[8] In fact, as O'Brien goes on to note, Paul sees such communities as proof of the reality of his calling. Paul would surely have appreciated the observation of John Wesley that Christianity was never meant to be a solitary religion.

Is this your vision of evangelism as a believer? Not simply the conversion of individuals but the building of a Christian community where new believers can be nurtured on the Word of God and grow into Christian maturity, where they can regularly partake of the Lord's Supper, that ordinance which so powerfully speaks of the corporate unity of believers in Christ, and where they can know the joys of Christian fellowship. Again, Paul would have heartily approved of those words in the *Second London Confession of Faith* (1677), where we are told that 'by their profession of faith', believers 'are committed to the maintenance of a holy fellowship and communion in the worship of God'.[9]

PLANS FOR MINISTRY
IN THE WESTERN MEDITERRANEAN

It was this ministry in the northeastern quadrant of the Mediterranean that had prevented Paul from coming to Rome before the writing of this letter (Rom. 15:22). But now he had come to the conviction that his pioneer ministry in this area was drawing to a close. How he knew this we are not told. But such a sense of direction has been given to other servants of God down through the years. When Martyn Lloyd-Jones, for instance, came to retire in 1968 from his marvellous ministry at Westminster Chapel in London he did so with a deep conviction that one phase of his ministry was being brought to an end and another was about to begin. He had undergone a serious operation for cancer that year, but this was, he later wrote, only 'a precipitating factor in what was becoming an increasing conviction'. When he discovered that he needed this operation, he said: 'I felt that God was saying to me, "This is the end of one ministry and the beginning of another".'[10] We do not know what factors God brought into Paul's life to convince the apostle that he 'no longer had a place in these parts' (Rom. 15:23), but the conviction appears to have been similar to that of Lloyd-Jones: God was bringing to an end one phase of his missionary work and launching him out into another.

As to the locality of the new ministry that Paul believed God was giving him, it was at the other end of the Mediterranean: Spain.[11] Whether or not the apostle ever set foot on Spanish soil is a matter of some debate among the commentators. The sixteenth-century

Reformer John Calvin felt that it is quite uncertain as to whether Paul reached Spain.[12] Thomas Scott (1747-1821), an evangelical Anglican commentator of the early nineteenth century, believed that he did. In support of his view, Scott cited an early Christian document known as *1 Clement*, written by an elder in the church at Rome towards the end of the first century, in which it is stated that Paul did journey as far as 'the limits of the west', that is, to Spain.[13]

It is more profitable and instructive, though, to look at the challenges upon which Paul must have reflected as he contemplated this new missionary undertaking. The Romans had begun the conquest of Spain in the third century B.C. and by Paul's day all of the country was firmly under Roman rule. But there were two major difficulties that he would have had to face in seeking to evangelize Spain.

First, there was the fact that until the third and fourth centuries A.D. there is no evidence at all of any substantial Jewish settlements or synagogues in Spain.[14] Yet, Paul's usual missionary strategy in the eastern Mediterranean had been to make the synagogue the *initial* place of evangelism when he came to establish a local church in a city. For example, when he went to Athens he first went to the synagogue to reason about Christ with the Jews and Gentile worshippers there (Acts 17:16-17). Invariably Paul would run into opposition in the synagogue, and he would eventually have to find another venue for evangelism. But it is clear from Acts that the synagogue was the first place that Paul sought to win a hearing for the gospel. This is quite understandable in view of the fact that Jesus, as the Messiah, fulfills all of the prophecies predicted about him throughout the Old Testament. Moreover, Paul and those who attended the synagogue reverenced the Old Testament Scriptures as a pure revelation from God, something that Greek and Roman pagans certainly did not do.

If there were no significant Jewish settlements at all in Spain, however, this method of evangelism would need to be changed. Paul had to have expected to begin his evangelistic ministry in totally pagan surroundings, where there was no devotion to the Old Testament and where there would be little, if any, initial interest in a proclamation that Jesus was the Messiah.[15]

Second, despite the fact that the country was ruled by the Romans and the Romans were consciously seeking to Romanize the peoples of the Iberian peninsula, in a number of places, especially the north, Roman civilization was only a veneer. Moreover, Greek, which was the language that Paul had primarily used in the eastern Mediterranean, was spoken in only a few pockets along the Mediterranean. Paul would have to have used Latin and, in those areas generally untouched by Roman culture, a translator who would have known the native languages.[16] If Paul focused his ministry on the relatively few Greek speakers in the country, it might impede the spread of the gospel. Proclamation and teaching would have to be done in Latin, which probably means that the apostle was fluent enough in this language to preach and teach. But there was, as far as we know, no translation of the Old Testament into Latin at this point. So Paul would have had to translate the Scriptures himself or had an assistant do it.[17]

In planning this mission to Spain, Paul was, therefore, contemplating something quite different from any of the missionary work he had hitherto undertaken. He was going into an utterly pagan environment where there would be substantial linguistic problems. Why was he doing this after two strenuous decades of ministry in the eastern Mediterranean where there was still much to be done?[18]

Well, first, there is his belief that his work in the east was winding down. Then, there is his firm conviction that comes to expression in 1 Corinthians 9:16: 'woe is me if I do not preach the gospel!' God's calling for Paul's life was that he be a preacher of the gospel to the Gentiles, especially in the northern Mediterranean, and if he refused to fulfill this calling he would know God's displeasure.[19]

But even more importantly, he knew that men and women, wherever they live and whatever race they belong to, have been created to glorify God. When, in Romans 1 Paul discusses some of the characteristics of sinful Gentile existence, almost the first one that he mentions is that fallen Gentiles fail to glorify God (Rom. 1:21). But, now through the death and resurrection of Jesus, the Lord of glory, Gentiles can glorify God, as Paul has written in Romans 15:

> Jesus Christ was a servant to the circumcision for the truth of God, to confirm the promises made to the fathers, and that the Gentiles might *glorify* God for his mercy; as it is written, 'For this reason I will confess to you among the Gentiles, and sing to your name.' And again he says, 'Rejoice, O Gentiles, with his people.' And again, 'Praise the Lord, all you Gentiles! Laud him, all you peoples!' And again, Isaiah says, 'There shall be a root of Jesse, and he who shall rise to reign over the Gentiles, in him the Gentiles shall hope' (Romans 15:8-12, *italics added*).

What was leading him to Spain was a divine compulsion to preach the gospel so that the elect among the Gentiles there might find the reason for their existence: 'to glorify God' and, we could rightly add in the words of the *Shorter Westminster Catechism*, 'to enjoy him for ever'. Or as the hymnwriter Charles Wesley (1707-1788) put it so well:

> Enlarge, inflame and fill my heart
>   With boundless charity divine:
> So shall I all my strength exert,
>   And love them with a zeal like Thine;
> And lead them to Thy open side,
>   The sheep for whom their Shepherd died.[20]

ENDNOTES

ACKNOWLEDGEMENTS

1   For a concise table of these elements, see Richard Lovelace, *Dynamics of Spiritual Life: An Evangelical Theology of Renewal* (Downers Grove, Illinois: InterVarsity Press, 1979), 75.

INTRODUCTION

1   John D. Woodbridge, 'Why Did Thomas Howard Become a Roman Catholic?', *Christianity Today*, 29, no.8 (1985), 49. There are two other parts to this special report: Randy Frame, 'Well-known Evangelical Author Thomas Howard Converts to Catholicism', *Christianity Today*, 29, no.8 (17 May 1985), 46-47 and John D. Woodbridge, 'Is Evangelical Faith Enough?', *Christianity Today* 29, no.8 (17 May 1985), 58-62. For a recent discussion of Howard's conversion, and that of other evangelicals, to Roman Catholicism, see Mark Noll and Carolyn Nystrom, 'Is the Reformation Over?', *Books & Culture*, 11, no.4 (July/August 2005), 16-18.

2   Richard Lovelace, *Renewal as a Way of Life* (Downers Grove, Illinois: InterVarsity Press, 1985), 15.

3   Edith M. Humphrey, 'It's Not About Us', *Christianity Today*, 45, no.5 (2 April 2001), 68.

4   Cited Walter Principe, 'Toward defining spirituality', *Studies in Religion*, 12, no.2 (Spring 1983), 130-131. According to T. R. Albin, the word owes its origin to

French Catholicism — he does not mention the French word, but presumably he is thinking of the word *spiritualité* — and it did not emerge as a 'well-defined branch of theology until the 18th century' ['Spirituality' in Sinclair B. Ferguson and David F. Wright, *New Dictionary of Theology* (Downers Grove, Illinois/Leicester, England: InterVarsity Press, 1988), 656].

5   On Ranew, see Chapter 7.

6   Nathanael Ranew, *Solitude Improved by Divine Meditation* (1839 ed.; repr. Morgan, Pennsylvania: Soli Deo Gloria, 1995), 98.

7   For reasons of space, certain areas of evangelical spirituality cannot be explored in this volume. For example, the role that the Lord's Table has played, and should play, in drawing near to God is not discussed. Evangelicals have rightly rejected the Roman Catholic view that the Mass is the central means by which we draw near to God. Historically, though, they have not been oblivious to the importance of the Lord's Table in kindling love for the triune God. See, for example, Michael A. G. Haykin, '"His soul-refreshing presence": The Lord's Supper in Calvinistic Baptist Thought and Experience in the "Long" Eighteenth Century' in Anthony R. Cross and Philip E. Thompson, eds., *Baptist Sacramentalism* (*Studies in Baptist History and Thought*, vol. 5; Carlisle, Cumbria/Waynesboro, Georgia: Paternoster Press, 2003), 177-193.

For a contemporary expression of the Roman Catholic view, see Joseph Ratzinger (Benedict XVI), *God Is Near Us. The Eucharist, The Heart of Life*, eds. Stephan Otto Horn and Vinzenz Pfnür and trans. Henry Taylor (San Francisco: Ignatius Press, 2003).

CHAPTER ONE: A TRINITARIAN SPIRITUALITY

1   William Carey, *An Enquiry into the Obligations of Christians, to Use Means for the Conversion of the Heathens* (Leicester, 1792), 8.

2   Carey, *Enquiry*, 8-13, quote from page 13. For an examination of the exegetical basis of Carey's understanding of Matthew 28:19-20, see Peter O'Brien, 'The Great Commission of Matthew 28:18-20. A Missionary Mandate or Not?', *The Reformed Theological Review*, 35 (1976), 66-78.

3   Gordon D. Fee, *God's Empowering Presence: The Holy Spirit in the Letters of Paul* (Peabody, Massachusetts: Hendrickson Publishers, 1994), 161-163.

4   Fee, *God's Empowering Presence*, 699-705.

5   See James D. G. Dunn, *Baptism in the Holy Spirit. A re-examination of the New Testament Teaching on the Gift of the Spirit in relation to Pentecostalism today* (London: SCM Press Ltd., 1970), 165-170. This early work by Dunn is an excellent resource. Areas of his later work involve much that is of questionable value.

6   Fee, *God's Empowering Presence*, 363.

7   Fee, *God's Empowering Presence*, 363-364. Other Pauline passages which could be mentioned include Galatians 4:6; 1 Thessalonians 1:2-5; 2 Thessalonians 2:13-14; Ephesians 2:18; 3:14-17.

8   Benjamin B. Warfield, 'The Biblical Doctrine of the Trinity' in his *Biblical Doctrines* (1929 ed.; repr. Edinburgh/Carlisle, Pennsylvania: The Banner of Truth Trust, 1988), 160.

9   For the identification of the 'seven Spirits' as a symbolic allusion to the Holy

Spirit, see Richard J. Bauckham, 'The Role of the Spirit in the Apocalypse', *The Evangelical Quarterly*, 52 (1980), 75-77; G. K. Beale, *The Book of Revelation* (Grand Rapids/Cambridge, U.K.: William B. Eerdmans Publ. Co./Carlisle, Cumbria: Paternoster Press, 1999), 189-190.

10 For a good discussion of the reliability of the trinitarian teaching of John's Gospel, see Millard J. Erickson, *God in Three Persons. A Contemporary Interpretation of the Trinity* (Grand Rapids: Baker Book House, 1995), 194-198.

11 D. A. Carson, *The Farewell Discourse and Final Prayer of Jesus. An Exposition of John 14-17* (Grand Rapids: Baker Book House, 1980), 49-50.

12 Warfield, 'Biblical Doctrine of the Trinity', 153.

13 See Alvyn Petersen, *Athanasius* (Ridgefield, Connecticut/Harrisburg, Pennsylvania: Morehouse Publishing, 1995), 186-189.

14 For a brief discussion of Modalism and its refutation, see Michael Haykin, 'Does God Wear Masks? Re-examining The Modalism Heresy', *The Evangelical Baptist*, 40, no.4 (February 1993), 16-17. This article has been essentially reprinted as an appendix in Michael A. G. Haykin, *Defence of the Truth: Contending for the truth yesterday and today* (Darlington: Evangelical Press, 2004), 125-129.

15 Warfield, 'Biblical Doctrine of the Trinity', 153-156.

16 J. I. Packer, 'The Trinity and the Gospel' in *Celebrating the Saving Work of God. The Collected Shorter Writings of J. I. Packer. Volume 1* (Carlisle, Cumbria: Paternoster Press, 1998), 7.

17 In A. M. Allchin, *Songs to Her God: Spirituality of Ann Griffiths* (Cambridge, Massachusetts: Cowley Publications, 1987), 93, altered.

18 This important insight is traceable to Basil of Caesarea, *Letter* 125.3.

19 For the transcript of this show, which aired on 29 September 2001, see www.cnn.com.

20 Cited Fee, *God's Empowering Presence*, 363.

21 Sadly, in his later life Watts himself shows some confusion in his convictions about the trinity. For a full discussion, see Arthur Paul Davis, *Isaac Watts: His Life and Works* (Published Ph.D. thesis, Columbia University, 1943), 109-126.

22 G. R. Beasley-Murray, *Baptism in the New Testament* (Grand Rapids: William B. Eerdmans Publ. Co., 1962), 91.

23 From the hymn 'Come, thou Almighty King' (author unknown).

CHAPTER TWO: KNOWING GOD AND KNOWING OURSELVES

1 Lovelace, *Renewal as a Way of Life: A Guidebook for Spiritual Growth* (Downers Grove, Illinois: InterVarsity Press, 1985), 18

2 Lovelace, *Renewal as a Way of Life*, 18-19. Classical Greek counsel was to 'Know thyself.' In some ways this is similar to contemporary western culture's emphasis on self-fulfillment. It should be noted, though, that the Greek maxim can be used in a thoroughly biblical manner. For instance, George Whitefield (1714-1770), in a sermon entitled 'Christ the Believer's Wisdom, Righteousness, Sanctification, and

Redemption' [*Sermons on Important Subjects* (London: Thomas Tegg, 1833), 502] sees 'true wisdom' in this maxim, for it directs people to know themselves as they truly are, namely sinners under the judgement of God. As such it points them to the true wisdom, which is Jesus Christ. He bases the latter on 1 Corinthians 1:30.

3 John Calvin, *Institutes* 1.1.2 [trans. Ford Lewis Battles in his and John T. McNeill, eds., *Calvin: Institutes of the Christian Religion. The Library of Christian Classics*, 20; (Philadelphia: Westminster Press, 1960), 37]. For the opening sentence of the French version of 1560, see Battles and McNeill, eds., *Institutes of the Christian Religion*, 36, n.3.

4 The quoted words are those of Lovelace: *Renewal as a Way of Life*, 20.

5 *Institutes* 1.1.3. Meditate, for example, on the following Scripture texts: Isaiah 6:1-5; Habakkuk 3:1-4, 16; Luke 5:1-5; and Revelation 1:12-18.

6 Lovelace, *Renewal as a Way of Life*, 24, 25-26.

7 In Psalm 19:1 this thought is taken one step further: 'The heavens declare the glory of God; and the sky above proclaims his handiwork.' The God with whom we have to deal is an all-powerful King, whose glory fills the entirety of his universe!

8 Lovelace, *Renewal as a Way of Life*, 21.

9 See Chapter 4.

10 Lovelace, *Renewal as a Way of Life*, 72; Anthony Thistleton, 'Flesh', in Colin Brown, ed., *The New International Dictionary of New Testament Theology* (Grand Rapids: Zondervan, 1975), I, 680.

11 Lovelace, *Renewal as a Way of Life*, 79.

12 For more detail on this, see below, Chapter 4.

13 *Of the Mortification of Sin in Believers* [*The Works of John Owen* (1850-1853 ed.; repr. Edinburgh/Carlisle, Pennsylvania: The Banner of Truth Trust, 1967), VI, 33, 86].

14 Lovelace, *Renewal as a Way of Life*, 73-74.

15 Kenneth Prior, *The Way of Holiness. A Study in Christian Growth* (Rev. ed.; Downers Grove, Illinois: InterVarsity Press, 1982), 37.

16 Sinclair B. Ferguson, 'The Reformed View' in Donald L. Alexander, ed., *Christian Spirituality: Five Views of Sanctification* (Downers Grove, Illinois: InterVarsity Press, 1988), 62.

17 Ferguson, 'Reformed View', 63.

18 Lovelace, *Renewal as a Way of Life*, 78-79.

19 Allen C. Guelzo, 'John Owen, Puritan Pacesetter', *Christianity Today*, 20, no.17 (21 May 1976), 14. For a study of Owen, see Michael A. G. Haykin, 'The Calvin of England: Some Aspects of the Life of John Owen (1616-1683) and his Teaching on Biblical Piety', *Reformed Baptist Theological Review*, 1, no.2 (July 2004), 169-183.

20 'Introduction' to James M. Houston, abr. and ed., *John Owen: Sin & Temptation: The Challenge to Personal Godliness* (Portland, Oregon: Multnomah Press, 1983), xxiv.

21 *Works of John Owen*, VI, 153-322.

22 *Works of John Owen*, VI, 87-151.

23 *Works of John Owen*, VI, 126.

24 *Works of John Owen*, VI, 1-86.

25 *Works of John Owen*, VI, 20. See also the comments of J. I. Packer, ' "Keswick"

and the Reformed Doctrine of Sanctification', *The Evangelical Quarterly*, 27 (1955), 156.

26 *Works of John Owen*, VI, 85.

27 *Works of John Owen*, VI, 188. For further discussion of this area of Owen's teaching, see Michael A. G. Haykin, 'The Great Beautifier of Souls', *The Banner of Truth*, 242 (November 1983), 18-22.

CHAPTER THREE: A CHRIST-CENTRED SPIRITUALITY

1 J. I. Packer, *Keep In Step With The Spirit* (Old Tappan, New Jersey: Fleming H. Revell Co., 1984), 64-65. A slightly revised edition was released by Zondervan in 2005.

2 *The Greatest Fight in the World* (London: Passmore and Alabaster, 1891), 64.

3 'Receiving the Holy Ghost' [*The Metropolitan Tabernacle Pulpit* (Repr. Pasadena, Texas: Pilgrim Publications, 1973), 29:395].

4 'Jesus, wondrous Saviour' in *Memoir of Daniel Arthur McGregor* (2nd ed.; Toronto: Dudley & Burns, 1891), 101-102.

5 *An Exposition of the Epistle to the Hebrews* [*The Works of John Owen* (1855 ed.; repr. Edinburgh/Carlisle, Pennsylvania: The Banner of Truth Trust, 1991), XXIII, 145].

6 *Hebrews* (*Works of John Owen*, XXIII, 145).

7 One recent study places the Exodus around 1446 B.C. See Lennart Möller, *The Exodus Case*, trans. Margaret Bäckman (Copenhagen: Scandinavia Publishing House, 2002), 196-204. For a full discussion of the issues involved in dating the Exodus, see R. K. Harrison, *Introduction to the Old Testament* (Grand Rapids: William B. Eerdmans, 1969), 174-177, 315-325.

8 For her life story, see Joyce Tyldesley, *Hatchepsut: The Female Pharaoh* (London: Viking, 1996). For the dates of her reign, see Ian Shaw and Paul Nicholson, *The Dictionary of Ancient Egypt* (Rev. ed.; New York: Harry N. Abrams, Inc., 2003), 120-121, 311.

9 Jacquetta Hawkes, *The First Great Civilizations* (London: Hutchinson & Co., 1973), 367.

10 *Hebrews* (*Works of John Owen*, XXIII, 147).

11 *Hebrews* (*Works of John Owen*, XXIII, 148).

12 *Hebrews* (*Works of John Owen*, XXIII, 149).

13 For an excellent website devoted to Ann's literary work and studies of her writings, life, and spirituality, see E. Wyn James, ed., 'Ann Griffiths Website' (www.anngriffiths.cf.ac.uk).

14 Cited A. M. Allchin, *Songs to Her God. Spirituality of Ann Griffiths* (Cambridge, Massachusetts: Cowley Publications, 1987), 113.

CHAPTER FOUR: A CROSS-CENTRED SPIRITUALITY

1 For another commentary on this story in the light of the cross, see Paul F. M. Zahl, *Who Will Deliver Us? The Present Power of the Death of Christ* (New York: The Seabury Press, 1983), 29-30.

2 For an overview of Marshall's life and career, see Henry Bonser, 'A Memoir

of the Author: Laurance Henry Marshall 1882-1953' in L. H. Marshall, *Rivals of the Christian Faith* (London: Carey Kingsgate Press, 1954), 1-15. For a clear statement of his theological convictions, see Marshall's 'Religious Controversy in Canada', *The Fraternal and Remembrancer*, N.S., 1 (January 1931), 6-11. On his theological views, see also Barry D. Smith, 'Was Laurence H. Marshall really a Modernist?' (Unpublished typescript ms., n.d., in the possession of the author).

3   Cp. Marshall, 'Religious Controversy in Canada', 10.

4   See also the report of a talk by Marshall in which he described Christ's death as that of a martyr: W. J. H. Brown, ['Modernism'] (Unpublished MS. W. Gordon Brown Papers, McMaster Divinity College Archives, McMaster University, Ontario), [4].

It needs to be noted that this perspective has reappeared among professing evangelicals. For instance, in October 2004, at a public gathering arranged by the Evangelical Alliance at Emmanuel Evangelical Church, Westminster, England, Steve Chalke, a prominent figure in English evangelical circles, delivered what has been described as 'an extraordinary attack on the doctrine of penal substitution'. He minced no words as he referred to this vital evangelical doctrine as 'cosmic child abuse', 'distorted', 'simplistic', and 'ethically weak'! He maintained that this biblical truth perpetuated 'the myth that violence can be redemptive'. As Jonathan Stephen rightly notes, Chalke's views are simply classic Liberalism ('Chalkegate', *Affinity magazine* [Autumn 2004], 4-5).

5   For the life and ministry of T. T. Shields, see especially Arnold Dallimore, 'T. T. Shields', *Reformation Today*, 86 (July-August 1985), 7-10; *idem*, 'Thomas Todhunter Shields: Baptist Fundamentalist' (Unpublished MS., n.d.; copy in the author's possession); G. A. Rawlyk, 'A. L. McCrimmon, H. P. Whidden, T. T. Shields, Christian Education, and McMaster University' in his ed., *Canadian Baptists and Christian Higher Education* (Kingston/Montreal: McGill-Queen's University Press, 1988), 31-62; Leslie K. Tarr, *Shields of Canada. T.T. Shields (1873-1955)* (Grand Rapids: Baker Book House, 1967); *idem*, 'Another Perspective on T. T. Shields and Fundamentalism' in Jarold K. Zeman, ed., *Baptists in Canada: Search for Identity Amidst Diversity* (Burlington, Ontario: G. R. Welch Co., Ltd., 1980), 209-224; *idem*, 'T. T. Shields: A Soldier in the Field', *Fundamentalist Journal*, 2, no.6 (June 1983), 42-44.

6   'Our Doctrinal Statement: Of the Atonement for Sin' in *Toronto Baptist Seminary and Bible College 2005/2006 Prospectus* (Toronto: Toronto Baptist Seminary and Bible College, 2005), 14.

7   On the reading *epathen* as opposed to *apethanen*, see Francis Wright Beare, *The First Epistle of Peter* (Oxford: Basil Blackwell, 1961), 141; Peter H. Davids, *The First Epistle of Peter* (Grand Rapids: William B. Eerdmans Publ. Co., 1990), 135, n.17; J. Ramsey Michaels, *1 Peter* (Waco, Texas: Word Books, 1988), 195.

8   See further Kenneth Grayston, *Dying We Live. A New Enquiry into the Death of Christ in the New Testament* (New York/Oxford: Oxford University Press, 1990), 249, 374-375.

9   Leon Morris, *The Cross in the New Testament* (Grand Rapids: William B. Eerdmans Publ. Co., 1965), 322-323.

10   Zahl, *Who Will Deliver Us?*, 42-43.

11   James Denney, *The Death of Christ* (London: The Tyndale Press, 1951), 62.

12 Denney, *Death of Christ*, 62.

13 Cf. Denney, *Death of Christ*, 62.

14 For crucicentrism as a key element of classical evangelicalism, see David Bebbington, *Evangelicalism in Modern Britain. A History from the 1730s to the 1980s* (1989 ed.; repr. Grand Rapids: Baker Book House, 1992), 14-17. Bebbington's thesis regarding the discontinuity between Puritanism and evangelicalism is not without its problems, but his point about crucicentrism as a hallmark of evangelical life and thought is surely correct.

15 David Bebbington, 'Evangelical Christianity and the Enlightenment', *Crux*, 25, no.4 (December 1989), 30.

16 See, for instance, 2 Corinthians 5:21. Imputation has frequently been a matter of controversy in the church. For instance, the eighteenth-century Scottish divine Robert Riccaltoun (1691-1769) notes of reactions in his day to theological uses of the word 'imputation': 'Some have taken such an aversion to the word, that they cannot bear the mention of it; while others show such an extraordinary fondness of the term, that no other form of words can please them where this is left out' [*Essays on Several of the Doctrines of Revelation* in *The Works of the Late Reverend Mr Robert Riccaltoun V1: Minister of the Gospel at Hobkirk* (Edinburgh: A. Murray & J. Cochran for the author's son, 1771), 305-306].

Recently, this issue of the imputation of the active obedience of Christ has again become an issue of controversy. For defences of the Reformed perspective on this issue, see John Piper, *Counted Righteous in Christ: Should We Abandon the Imputation of Christ's Righteousness?* (Wheaton, Illinois: Crossway Books, 2002) and Brian J. Vickers, *Jesus' Blood and Righteousness: Paul's Theology of Imputation* (Wheaton, Illinois: Crossway Books, 2006).

17 Cited M. Eugene Osterhaven, *The Faith of the Church. A Reformed Perspective on its Historical Development* (Grand Rapids: William B. Eerdmans Publishing Co., 1982), 109-110.

18 G. W. Bromiley, 'The Doctrine of Justification in Luther', *The Evangelical Quarterly*, 24 (1952), 98-99.

19 Michael S. Horton, 'The Sola's of the Reformation' in James Montgomery Boice and Benjamin E. Sasse, eds., *Here We Stand! A Call from Confessing Evangelicals for a Modern Reformation* (Grand Rapids: Baker Books, 1996), 123.

20 Cited Alasdair I. C. Heron, *The Holy Spirit* (Philadelphia: Westminster Press, 1983), 100.

CHAPTER FIVE: A SPIRITUALITY OF THE WORD

1 Benjamin Francis, *Circular Letter of the Western Association* (n.p., 1778), 2.

2 This story is told by Stephen Farris, *The Preaching That Matters: The Bible and Our Lives* (Louisville: Westminster/John Knox Press, 1998), 147.

3 See, for example, Proverbs 30:5: Luke 11:28; Acts 13:5. In Romans 3:2, Paul refers to the Old Testament Scriptures as 'the very words of God'.

4 J. I. Packer, *'Fundamentalism' and the Word of God: Some Evangelical Principles* (London: Inter-Varsity Fellowship, 1958), 80.

5   Some of what follows is drawn from Michael A. G. Haykin, 'William Tyndale: The Father Of The English Bible', *The Evangelical Baptist*, 41, no.11 (October 1994), 14-16. Used by permission.

6   Cited John Capon, 'New home for Tyndale's 1526 New Testament', *Baptist Times* (5 May 1994), 15.

7   For the story of its being found, see 'Good news from Stuttgart: A hitherto unrecorded copy of the first complete printing of William Tyndale's English translation of the New Testament', Württembergische Landesbibliothek Stuttgart (www.wlb-stuttgart.de/english/tyndalee.html; accessed 6 June 2004).

8   'Good news from Stuttgart.'

9   *The Encyclopædia Britannica* (11th ed.; New York: Encyclopædia Britannica, Inc., 1911), XXVII, 499. The definitive biography of Tyndale is that of David Daniell, *William Tyndale. A Biography* (New Haven/London: Yale University Press, 1994).

10   'Prologue' to Genesis in G. E. Duffield, ed., *The Work of William Tyndale* (Appleford, Berkshire: The Sutton Courtenay Press, 1964), 37.

11   Daniell, *William Tyndale*, 3. See also Iain Murray, 'William Tyndale' (Lecture at Ebenezer Free Reformed Church, Dundas, Ontario, 24 October 1994).

12   For an excellent evaluation of Fox's life and thought, see Gaius Davies, 'George Fox: a Radical Spirit' in the *Fire Divine. Papers read at the 1996 Westminster Conference* (London: The Westminster Conference, 1996), 52-72. For a sympathetic study of Fox, see H. Larry Ingle, *First Among Friends: George Fox and the Creation of Quakerism* (New York/Oxford: Oxford University Press, 1994).

13   Cited Barry Reay, *The Quakers and the English Revolution* (New York: St. Martin's Press, 1985), 33. For a discussion of Fisher's approach to Scripture, see Dean Freiday, *The Bible: Its Criticism, Interpretation and Use in 16th and 17th Century England* (Pittsburgh: Catholic and Quaker Studies, 1979), 97-102. The substance of this and the next three paragraphs has already appeared in Michael A. G. Haykin, *Kiffin, Knollys and Keach: Rediscovering Our English Baptist Heritage* (Leeds: Reformation Today Trust, 1996), 65-67. Used by permission.

14   Cited Reay, *Quakers*, 34.

15   'Penington, Isaac (the Younger)' in Richard L. Greaves and Robert Zaller, eds., *Biographical Dictionary of British Radicals in the Seventeenth Century* (Brighton, Sussex: The Harvester Press, 1984), III, 23.

16   *Letters of Isaac Penington* (2nd ed.; repr. London: Holdsworth and Ball, 1829), 202-203. For access to these letters I am indebted to Heinz G. Dschankilic of Cambridge, Ontario.

17   See also the remarks by Richard Dale Land, 'Doctrinal Controversies of English Particular Baptists (1644-1691) as Illustrated by the Career and Writings of Thomas Collier' (Unpublished D.Phil. thesis, Regent's Park College, Oxford University, 1979), 205-211.

18   Cited Geoffrey F. Nuttall, *The Holy Spirit in Puritan Faith and Experience* (2nd ed.; Oxford: Basil Blackwell, 1947), 32.

19   *TROPOLOGIA: A Key to Open Scripture-Metaphors* (London: Enoch Prosser, 1681), II, 312.

20   William L. Lumpkin, *Baptist Confessions of Faith* (Rev. ed.; Valley Forge, Pennsylvania: Judson Press, 1969), 250.

21   For further reading on the debate between the Puritans and the Quaker over the relationship between the Scriptures and the Holy Spirit, see Peter Adam, *Word and Spirit: The Puritan-Quaker Debate* (London: St Antholin's Lectureship, 2001).

CHAPTER SIX: PRAYER AND THE CHRISTIAN LIFE

1   On Andrew Bonar, see especially Marjory Bonar, ed., *Andrew A. Bonar: Diary and Life* (1893 ed.; repr. Edinburgh: The Banner of Truth Trust, 1984); Alastair Morrice, 'Andrew Bonar: Reflections on his Diary', *The Rutherford Journal of Church & Ministry* 2, no.1 (Spring 1995), 18-20; Marjory Bonar, ed., *Andrew A. Bonar: The Good Pastor* (Belfast/Greenville, S. Carolina: Ambassador Publications, 1999). For a website devoted to the life and works of Andrew Bonar, see www.newblehome. co.uk/bonar; accessed 12 July 2007.

2   Cited David M. MacIntyre, *The Hidden Life of Prayer* (Tain, Ross-shire: Christian Focus Publications, 1989), xiii.

3   Gordon P. Wiles, *Paul's Intercessory Prayers. The Significance of the Intercessory Prayer Passages in the Letters of St Paul* (Cambridge: Cambridge University Press, 1974), 266.

4   Wiles, *Paul's Intercessory Prayers*, 81.

5   For similar statements, see 1 Thessalonians 5:25; 2 Corinthians 1:8-11; Ephesians 6:18-19; Colossians 4:2-4.

6   *A short forme of catechizing* in *Workes of R. Greenham* (5th ed.; London, 1612), 237-238. For an excellent study of Greenham's life and ministry, see John H. Primus, *Richard Greenham: Portrait of an Elizabethan Pastor* (Macon, Georgia: Mercer University Press, 1998). My attention was drawn to Greenham's statement on prayer by Primus, *Richard Greenham*, 138.

7   C. E. B. Cranfield, *A Critical and Exegetical Commentary on the Epistle to the Romans* (1979 ed.; repr. Edinburgh: T. & T. Clark, 1986), II, 776.

8   Cited MacIntyre, *The Hidden Life of Prayer*, 20.

9   *The Return of Prayers* [*The Works of Thomas Goodwin, D.D.* (Edinburgh: James Nichol, 1861), III, 362].

10   Letter to Charles Stuart, 1798, in Michael A. G. Haykin, ed., *The armies of the Lamb: The spirituality of Andrew Fuller* (Dundas, Ontario: Joshua Press, 2001), 62-64.

11   Gordon D. Fee, *God's Empowering Presence: The Holy Spirit in the Letters of Paul* (Peabody, Massachusetts: Hendrickson, 1994), 632.

12   *The Epistle to the Romans. Volume II: Chapters 9 to 16* [(The New International Commentary on the New Testament (Grand Rapids: William B. Eerdmans Publ. Co, 1965), 221].

13   *The Epistles of Paul to the Romans and to the Thessalonians* [trans. Ross Mackenzie (1960 ed.; repr. Grand Rapids: Wm. B. Eerdmans Publ. Co., 1973), 317]. See also Fee, *God's Empowering Presence*, 633.

14   Samuel Zwemer (1867-1952), cited D. A. Carson, *A Call to Spiritual Reformation:*

Priorities from Paul and His Prayers (Grand Rapids: Baker Books/Nottingham, UK: InterVarsity Press, 1992), 210 .

15 'Exhortation to Prayer' in John D. Baird and Charles Ryskamp, eds., *The Poems of William Cowper* (Oxford: Clarendon Press, 1980), I, 169.

16 *John Bunyan: The Doctrine of the Law and Grace unfolded and I will pray with the Spirit*, Richard L. Greaves, ed. (Oxford: Clarendon Press, 1976), 256-257. For a modern edition of this work, see John Bunyan, *Prayer* (Edinburgh: The Banner of Truth Trust, 1965). For a modernization and abridgment of it, see Louis Gifford Parkhurst, Jr. ed., *Pilgrim's Prayer Book* (Wheaton, Illinois: Tyndale House Publishers, Inc., 1986).

17 Bunyan, *I will pray with the Spirit*, 259.

18 *A Discourse of the Work of the Holy Spirit in Prayer* (1682) [William H. Goold , ed., *The Works of John Owen* (1850-1853 ed.; repr. Edinburgh: The Banner of Truth Trust, 1967), IV, 292-293]. For a helpful study of Owen's understanding of prayer, see Sinclair B. Ferguson, *John Owen on the Christian Life* (Edinburgh: The Banner of Truth Trust, 1987), 224-231.

19 For an exposition of this text, see Chapter 9.

20 *The River of Life Impeded* in his *Sermons on Various Subjects* (London: J. Burditt, 1806), 183-184.

CHAPTER SEVEN: CHRISTIAN MEDITATION

1 On the relationship between Word and Spirit, see Chapter 5.

2 Eugene Peterson, *Eat this Book: The Holy Community at Table with Holy Scripture* (Vancouver: Regent College Publishing, 2000), 9.

3 For what follows on meditation I am deeply indebted to Nigel Westhead, 'Christian Meditation', *The Rutherford Journal of Church & Ministry*, 3, no.1 (Spring 1996), 11-13. See also Simon K. H. Chan, 'The Puritan Meditative Tradition, 1599-1691: A Study of Ascetical Piety' (Unpublished D.Phil. thesis, Magdalene College, Cambridge University, 1986); Joel R. Beeke, 'The Puritan Practice of Meditation' in his *Puritan Reformed Spirituality* (Grand Rapids: Reformation Heritage Books, 2004), 73-100; and Stephen Yuille, '"Puritan meditation": The gateway from the head to the heart', *Eusebeia: The Bulletin of The Jonathan Edwards Centre for Reformed Spirituality*, 4 (Spring 2005), 7-16.

4 *Discussions of Robert Louis Dabney* (1891 ed.; repr. Edinburgh: The Banner of Truth Trust, 1982), 1:645-646. Compare in this regard Psalm 19:14; 77:6.

5 *The Sermons of Thomas Watson* (Ligonier, Pennsylvania: Soli Deo Gloria, 1990), 200-201.

6 Simon Chan, *Spiritual Theology: A Systematic Study of the Christian Life* (Downers Grove, Illinois: InterVarsity Press, 1998), 162.

7 In C. Frederick Barbee and Paul F. M. Zahl, compiled, *The Collects of Thomas Cranmer* (Grand Rapids/Cambridge, U.K.: William B. Eerdmans Publ. Co., 1999), 4.

8 Nathanael Ranew says of the text in Luke 2: Mary is 'the remarkable and special example of meditation mentioned...in the New Testament: we have none so punctual and plain...as this' [*Solitude Improved by Divine Meditation* (1839 ed.; repr.

Morgan, Pennsylvania: Soli Deo Gloria, 1995), 7].

9 Ranew, *Solitude Improved by Divine Meditation*, 24-25.

10 James W. Sire, *Habits of the Mind: Intellectual Life as a Christian Calling* (Downers Grove, Illinois: InterVarsity Press, 2000), 154.

11 Cited Westhead, 'Christian Meditation', 12.

12 Ranew, *Solitude Improved by Divine Meditation*, 42.

13 Ranew, *Solitude Improved by Divine Meditation*, 45.

14 Ranew, *Solitude Improved by Divine Meditation*, 72, 73.

15 See also Joshua 1:8 in this regard.

16 *Sermons of Thomas Watson*, 240, 243.

17 See Chapter 5.

18 *The True Excellency of a Gospel Minister* [*The Works of Jonathan Edwards* (1834 ed.; repr. Edinburgh: The Banner of Truth Trust, 1974), 2:959].

19 'The Life and Character of the Late Reverend Mr Jonathan Edwards' in David Levin, ed., *Jonathan Edwards: A Profile* (New York: Hill and Wang, 1969), 39.

20 For a recent edition of the *Resolutions*, see Stephen J. Nichols, ed., *Jonathan Edwards' Resolutions And Advice to Young Converts* (Phillipsburg, New Jersey: P&R Publishing, 2001). The *Resolutions* can be found on pages 17-26.

21 'Life and Character of the Late Reverend Mr Jonathan Edwards' in Levin, ed., *Jonathan Edwards*, 7.

22 My attention was drawn to this Resolution by John Piper, 'Saturate...Search', *The Standard* (March 1986), 36.

23 *The True Excellency of a Gospel Minister* (*Works*, 2:959).

24 *Personal Narrative* [*Letters and Personal Writings*, George S. Claghorn, ed., *The Works of Jonathan Edwards* (New Haven/ London: Yale University Press, 1998), 16, 797].

25 Cited 'Life and Character of the Late Reverend Mr Jonathan Edwards' in Levin, ed., *Jonathan Edwards*, 40-41.

26 Stephen J. Stein, 'The Spirit and the Word: Jonathan Edwards and Scriptural Exegesis' in Nathan O. Hatch and Harry S. Stout, eds., *Jonathan Edwards and the American Experience* (New York/Oxford: Oxford University Press, 1988), 121.

CHAPTER EIGHT: SPIRITUAL FRIENDSHIP AS A MEANS OF GRACE

1 An earlier version of this chapter appeared as 'On Friendship', *Reformation Today*, 140 (July-Aug 1994), 26-30. Used by permission.

2 Diogenes Allen, *Love: Christian Romance, Marriage, Friendship* (Cambridge, Massachusetts: Cowley Publications, 1987), 45-46.

3 *The Screwtape Letters*, Letter 10 in *The Best of C. S. Lewis* (Washington, D.C.: Canon Press, 1969), 43.

4 For example, in Proverbs 17:17, we read that 'a friend loves at all times' and Proverbs 18:24 tells us that there is 'a friend who sticks closer than a brother'. See also Proverbs 19:4,6; 22:11; 27:6,9-10,14,17. For an excellent study of some of these proverbs, see Bruce Waltke, 'Friends and Friendship in the Book of Proverbs: An

Exposition of Proverbs 27:1-11', *Crux*, 38, no.3 (September 2002), 27-42.

5   'Friendship', *Dictionary of Biblical Imagery*, Leland Ryken *et al*, eds. (Downers Grove, Illinois: InterVarsity Press, 1998), 308-309.

6   See also 1 Samuel 18:3.

7   R. Paul Stevens, 'Friendship' in Robert Banks and R. Paul Stevens, eds., *The Complete Book of Everyday Christianity* (Downers Grove, Illinois: InterVarsity Press, 1997), 439.

8   F. F. Bruce, *Paul: Apostle of the Heart Set Free* (Grand Rapids: William B. Eerdmans Publishing Co., 1977), 457.

9   Bruce, *Paul: Apostle of the Heart Set Free*, 457.

10   *The Autobiography of William Jay*, eds. George Redford and John Angell James (1854 ed.; repr. Edinburgh: The Banner of Truth Trust, 1974), 372, 373. For help in writing this paragraph I am indebted to the thought of Maurice Roberts, *The Thought of God* (Edinburgh: The Banner of Truth Trust, 1993), 175-176.

11   Roberts, *Thought of God*, 176.

12   Carolinne White, *Christian Friendship in the Fourth Century* (Cambridge: Cambridge University Press, 1992), 57.

13   *De vita sua* 225ff. [trans. Denise Molaise Meehan, *Saint Gregory of Nazianzus: Three Poems*, The Fathers of the Church, vol. 75 (Washington, D.C.: The Catholic University of America Press, 1987), 83-84].

14   Cited White, *Christian Friendship*, 70.

15   Richard Stauffer, *The Humanness of John Calvin* [trans. George H. Shriver (Nashville: Abingdon Press, 1971), 47].

16   Cited Stauffer, *Humanness of Calvin*, 57.

17   The earliest memoir of Ryland is that found at the conclusion of the sermon Robert Hall, Jr (1761-1834) preached at Ryland's funeral: 'A Sermon Occasioned by the death of the Rev. John Ryland, D.D., preached at the Baptist Meeting, Broadmead, Bristol, June 5, 1825', in Olinthus Gregory and Joseph Belcher, eds., *The Works of the Rev. Robert Hall, A. M.* (New York: Harper & Brothers, 1854), I, 213-224. Later in the nineteenth century, James Culross devoted a significant section of his *The Three Rylands: A hundred years of various Christian service* (London: Elliot Stock, 1897) to recounting the life and ministry of John Ryland, Jr (69-91). More recently, see Grant Gordon, 'John Ryland, Jr (1753-1825)' in Michael A. G. Haykin, ed., *The British Particular Baptists, 1638-1910* (Springfield, Missouri: Particular Baptist Press, 2000), 76-95.

An examination of Ryland's theology may be found in the excellent study by L. G., Champion, 'The Theology of John Ryland: Its Sources and Influences', *The Baptist Quarterly*, 28 (1979-1980), 17-29. Champion has also studied the significant friendship between Ryland and John Newton in his 'The Letters of John Newton to John Ryland', *The Baptist Quarterly*, 27 (1977-1978), 157-163.

18   For Fuller's life, the classic study is that of John Ryland, *The Work of Faith, the Labour of Love, and the Patience of Hope Illustrated; in the Life and Death of the Reverend Andrew Fuller* (London: Button & Son, 1816). A second edition of this biography was published by the same publisher in 1818: *The Work of Faith, the Labour of Love, and the Patience of Hope, illustrated; in the Life and Death of the Rev. Andrew Fuller*, henceforth

cited as *Life and Death of the Rev. Andrew Fuller* (2nd ed.).

For more recent studies, see Phil Roberts, 'Andrew Fuller' in Timothy George and David S. Dockery, eds., *Baptist Theologians* (Nashville: Broadman Press, 1990), 121-139; Peter J. Morden, *Offering Christ to the World: Andrew Fuller (1754-1815) and the Revival of Eighteenth-Century Particular Baptist Life* (Carlisle, Cumbria U.K./ Waynesboro, Georgia: Paternoster Press, 2003); and Michael A. G. Haykin, ed., *'At the Pure Fountain of Thy Word': Andrew Fuller as an Apologist* (Carlisle, Cumbria, U.K./Waynesboro, Georgia: Paternoster Press, 2004).

19 *The Indwelling and Righteousness of Christ no Security against Corporeal Death, but the Source of Spiritual and Eternal Life* (London: W. Button & Son, 1815), 2-3.

20 The Spurgeon remark is taken from Gilbert Laws, *Andrew Fuller: Pastor, Theologian, Ropeholder* (London: Carey Press, 1942), 127; A. C. Underwood, *A History of the English Baptists* (London: The Baptist Union Publication Dept., Kingsgate Press, 1947), 166.

21 *Memoir of the Life, Labors, and Extensive Usefulness of the Rev. Christmas Evans* (New York: M. W. Dodd, 1843), 74.

22 *Indwelling and Righteousness of Christ*, 1-2.

23 *Indwelling and Righteousness of Christ*, 36-37.

24 *Life and Death of the Rev. Andrew Fuller* (2nd ed.), viii-ix.

25 For this now obsolete meaning of the word 'tedious', see *The Oxford English Dictionary, s.v.*

26 'Laughing the Night Away', *Christianity Today*, 37, no.3 (8 March 1993), 15.

27 *Indwelling and Righteousness of Christ*, 35.

28 See Robinson, 'Laughing the Night Away', 15.

29 For the details, see E. Daniel Potts, '"I throw away the guns to preserve the ship": A Note on the Serampore Trio', *The Baptist Quarterly*, 20 (1963-1964), 115-117.

30 William Carey *et. al.*, Letter to the Baptist Missionary Society, 6 August 1805 (cited Potts, 'I throw away the guns', 116).

31 *Life and Death of the Rev. Andrew Fuller* (2nd ed.), ix-x.

32 Cited Ryland, *Indwelling and Righteousness of Christ*, 33.

33 Diary entry for 2 January 1759, *The Deserted Village. The Diary of an Oxfordshire Rector: James Newton of Nuneham Courtenay 1736-86* [transcribed and ed. Gavin Hannah (Stroud, Gloucestershire/Dover, New Hampshire: Alan Sutton, 1992), 2].

CHAPTER NINE: MISSION — THE INEVITABLE FRUIT OF TRUE SPIRITUALITY

1 See the excellent admonition with regard to this heritage by Peter Masters, 'The Battle for Souls', *Sword & Trowel*, no.2 (2005), 7-15.

2 Cited Mike Nicholls, *C. H. Spurgeon: The Pastor Evangelist* (London: The Baptist Historical Society, 1992), 97.

3 *The Promise of the Spirit, the Grand Encouragement in Promoting the Gospel [The Complete Works of the Rev. Andrew Fuller* (Repr. Harrisonburg, Virginia: Sprinkle

Publications, 1988), III, 359].

4   John Bunyan, *Grace Abounding to the Chief of Sinners* [W. R. Owens, ed. (Harmondsworth, Middlesex: Penguin Books Ltd., 1987), 72-73].

5   When Paul preached in Illyricum is not known. The term *kyklō* may then mean 'up to', that is, 'up to the border of Illyricum'.

6   W. P. Bowers, 'Mission' in Gerald F. Hawthorne, Ralph P. Martin, and Daniel G. Reid, eds., *Dictionary of Paul and His Letters* (Downers Grove, Illinois/Leciester: InterVarsity Press, 1993), 612.

7   Bowers, 'Mission', 609.

8   P. T. O'Brien, *Gospel and Mission in the Writings of Paul An Exegetical and Theological Analysis* (Grand Rapids: Baker/Carlisle, United Kingdom: Paternoster Press, 1995), 42.

9   *The Second London Confession of Faith* 27.2 [*A Faith to Confess: The Baptist Confession of Faith of 1689* (4th ed.; Haywards Heath, Sussex: Carey Publications Ltd., 1982), 60].

10   *Letters 1991-1981.* Selected Iain H. Murray (Edinburgh: The Banner of Truth Trust, 1994), 214.

11   It is noteworthy that Paul's ministry is still focused on the northern Mediterranean. James D. G. Dunn thus thinks it quite probable that 'Paul's grand design was to cover the northern half of the Mediterranean while others covered the southern half' [*Romans 9-16 (Word Biblical Commentary*, vol. 38B; 1988 ed.; repr. Milton Keynes: Word (UK) Ltd., 1991), 872].

12   John Calvin, *The Epistles of Paul the Apostle to the Romans and to the Thessalonians,* trans. Ross Mackenzie (1960 ed.; repr. Grand Rapids: Wm. B. Eerdmans Publishing Co., 1973), 314.

13   Thomas Scott, *The Holy Bible* (Boston: Crocker and Brewster, 1858), VI, 107. On the phrase 'the limits of the west' as a reference to Spain or possibly Gaul, see E. Earle Ellis, '"The End of the Earth" (Acts 1:8)', *Bulletin of Biblical Research*, 1 (1991), 129.

14   Robert Jewett, 'Paul, Phoebe, and the Spanish Mission' in Jacob Neusner, ed., *The Social World of Formative Christianity and Judaism* (Philadelphia: Fortress Press, 1988), 143-144.

15   Jewett, 'Paul, Phoebe, and the Spanish Mission', 144.

16   Jewett, 'Paul, Phoebe, and the Spanish Mission', 145-146.

17   Jewett, 'Paul, Phoebe, and the Spanish Mission', 146-147.

18   Romans 15:23 should not be understood to mean that there was nowhere else in the north-eastern Mediterranean where Paul could preach and that he had evangelized every last town and village in the area. Rather, he is indicating that he had fulfilled the mandate of his ministry in this area, which was to establish stable churches in key centres that could then evangelize surrounding towns and villages.

19   See the discussion of this verse by Gordon D. Fee, *The First Epistle to the Corinthians* (Grand Rapids: William B. Eerdmans Publishing Co., 1987), 418-419.

20   My attention was drawn to this verse by its inclusion in Jill Masters, *Building an Outreach Sunday School. A Lessons for Life Manual* (London: The Wakeman Trust, 2005), 5.

Select
BIBLIOGRAPHY

A select number of titles that have been referred to in the body of the book are included here as well as a few other titles that can be read or referred to with great profit.

GENERAL

Chan, Simon. *Spiritual Theology: A Systematic Study of the Christian Life* (Downers Grove, Illinois: InterVarsity Press, 1998).

Di Gangi, Mariano, *Great Themes in Puritan Preaching* (Guelph, Ontario: Joshua Press Inc., 2007)

Lovelace, Richard. *Dynamics of Spiritual Life: An Evangelical Theology of Renewal* (Downers Grove, Illinois: InterVarsity Press, 1979).

Lovelace, Richard. *Renewal as a Way of Life* (Downers Grove, Illinois: InterVarsity Press, 1985).

Packer, J. I. *Keep In Step With The Spirit* (Old Tappan, New Jersey: Fleming H. Revell Co., 1984).

Pipa, Jr., Joseph A. and J. Andrew Wortman, eds. *Reformed*

Spirituality: Communing with Our Glorious God (Taylors, South Carolina: Southern Presbyterian Press, Greenville Presbyterian Theological Seminary, 2003).

TRINITARIAN SPIRITUALITY

Bray, Gerald. *The Doctrine of God* (Downers Grove, Illinois: InterVarsity Press, 1993).

Haykin, Michael A. G. 'Knowing and Adoring the Triune God', *The Gospel Witness*, 80, no.7 (January 2002), 8-12.

Haykin, Michael A. G. *Defence of the Truth: Contending for the truth yesterday and today* (Darlington: Evangelical Press, 2004), 69-89.

Stirling, Andrew, ed. *The Trinity: An Essential for Faith in Our Time* (Nappanee, Indiana: Evangel Publishing House, 2002).

Toon, Peter. *Our Triune God: A Biblical Portrayal of the Trinity* (Wheaton, Illinois: Victor Books, 1996).

Warfield, Benjamin B. 'The Biblical Doctrine of the Trinity' in his *Biblical Doctrines* (1929 ed.; repr. Edinburgh/Carlisle, Pennsylvania: The Banner of Truth Trust, 1988), 131-172.

KNOWING GOD AND KNOWING OURSELVES

Haykin, Michael A. G. 'The Great Beautifier of Souls', *The Banner of Truth*, 242 (November 1983), 18-22.

Owen, John. *Of the Mortification of Sin in Believers* [William H. Goold, ed., *The Works of John Owen* (1850-1853 ed.; repr. Edinburgh/Carlisle, Pennsylvania: The Banner of Truth Trust, 1967), IV, 1-86].

Packer, J. I. '"Keswick" and the Reformed Doctrine of Sanctification', *The Evangelical Quarterly*, 27 (1955), 153-167.

Prior, Kenneth. *The Way of Holiness. A Study in Christian Growth* (Rev. ed.; Downers Grove, Illinois: InterVarsity Press, 1982).

JESUS CHRIST AND THE HOLY SPIRIT

Fee, Gordon D. *God's Empowering Presence: The Holy Spirit in the Letters of Paul* (Peabody, Massachusetts: Hendrickson, 1994).

Hurtado, Larry W. *Lord Jesus Christ. Devotion to Jesus in Earliest*

Christianity (Grand Rapids, Michigan/Cambridge, U.K.: William B. Eerdmans Publ. Co., 2003).

Nuttall, Geoffrey F. *The Holy Spirit in Puritan Faith and Experience* (2nd ed.; Oxford: Basil Blackwell, 1947).

THE CROSS

De Valdés, Juan and Don Benedetto. *The Benefit of Christ. Living Justified because of Christ's Death*, abridged and ed. James M. Houston (1984 ed.; repr. Vancouver, British Columbia: Regent College Publishing, 2003).

Morris, Leon. *The Cross in the New Testament* (Grand Rapids: William B. Eerdmans Publ. Co., 1965).

Packer, J. I. 'Sola Fide: The Reformed Doctrine of Justification' in R. C. Sproul, ed., *Soli Deo Gloria: Essays in reformed Theology. Festschrift for John H. Gerstner* (Phillipsburg, New Jersey: P&R Publishing Co., 1976), 11-25.

Packer, J. I. *Celebrating the Saving Work of God* [*The Collected Shorter Writings of J. I. Packer*, vol. 1 (Carlisle, Cumbria: Paternoster Press, 1998)].

Piper, John. *Counted Righteous in Christ: Should We Abandon the Imputation of Christ's Righteousness?* (Wheaton, Illinois: Crossway Books, 2002).

Turretin, Francis. *Justification* [trans. George Musgrave Giger and ed. James T. Dennison, Jr. (Phillipsburg, New Jersey: P&R Publishing Co., 2004)].

Vickers, Brian J. *Jesus' Blood and Righteousness: Paul's Theology of Imputation* (Wheaton, Illinois: Crossway Books, 2006).

Zahl, Paul F. M. *Who Will Deliver Us? The Present Power of the Death of Christ* (New York: The Seabury Press, 1983).

WORD-CENTRED SPIRITUALITY

Adam, Peter. *Word and Spirit: The Puritan-Quaker Debate* (London: St Antholin's Lectureship, 2001).

Campbell, John Wesley. 'John Owen's Rule and Guide: A Study in the Relationship between the Word and the Spirit in the

Thought of Dr John Owen' (Unpublished Th.M. thesis, Regent College, Vancouver, British Columbia, 1991).

Haykin, Michael A. G. 'William Tyndale: The Father Of The English Bible', *The Evangelical Baptist*, 41, no.11 (October 1994), 14-16.

Packer, J. I. *'Fundamentalism' and the Word of God: Some Evangelical Principles* (London: Inter-Varsity Fellowship, 1958).

Peterson, Eugene. *Eat this Book: The Holy Community at Table with Holy Scripture* (Vancouver: Regent College Publishing, 2000).

PRAYER

Bakker, Frans. *Praying Always*, trans. Cornelis and Frederika Pronk (Edinburgh: The Banner of Truth Trust, 1987).

Andrew A. Bonar: Diary and Life, ed. Marjory Bonar (1893 ed.; repr. Edinburgh: The Banner of Truth Trust, 1984).

Bryant, David. *With Concerts of Prayer* (Ventura, California: Regal Books, 1984).

Bunyan, John. *I will pray with the Spirit* in *John Bunyan: The Doctrine of the Law and Grace unfolded and I will pray with the Spirit*, ed. Richard L. Greaves (Oxford: Clarendon Press, 1976).

Carson, D. A. *A Call to Spiritual Reformation: Priorities from Paul and His Prayers* (Grand Rapids: Baker Books/Nottingham, UK: InterVarsity Press, 1992).

Hunter, W. Bingham. *The God Who Hears* (Downers Grove, Illinois: InterVarsity Press, 1986).

MacIntyre, David M. *The Hidden Life of Prayer* (Tain, Ross-shire: Christian Focus Publications, 1989).

Owen, John. *A Discourse of the Work of the Holy Spirit in Prayer* (1682) [William H. Goold, ed., *The Works of John Owen* (1850-1853 ed.; repr. Edinburgh/Carlisle, Pennsylvania: The Banner of Truth Trust, 1967), IV, 235-350].

Whitney, Donald S. *Spiritual Disciplines for the Christian Life* (Colorado Springs: NavPress, 1991), 61-78.

Whitney, Donald S. *Spiritual Disciplines Within the Church* (Colorado Springs: NavPress, 1996), 163-175.

MEDITATION

Beeke, Joel R. 'The Puritan Practice of Meditation' in his *Puritan Reformed Spirituality* (Grand Rapids: Reformation Heritage Books, 2004), 73-100.

Chan, Simon K. H. 'The Puritan Meditative Tradition, 1599-1691: A Study of Ascetical Piety' (Unpublished D.Phil. thesis, Magdalene College, Cambridge University, 1986).

Ranew, Nathaniel. *Solitude Improved by Divine Meditation* (1839 ed.; repr. Morgan, Pennsylvania: Soli Deo Gloria, 1995).

Roberts, Maurice. *The Thought of God* (Edinburgh: The Banner of Truth Trust, 1993).

Westhead, Nigel. 'Christian Meditation', *The Rutherford Journal of Church & Ministry*, 3, no.1 (Spring 1996), 11-13.

Yuille, Stephen. '"Puritan meditation": The gateway from the head to the heart', *Eusebeia: The Bulletin of The Jonathan Edwards Centre for Reformed Spirituality*, 4 (Spring 2005), 7-16.

FRIENDSHIP

'Friendship', *Dictionary of Biblical Imagery*, eds. Leland Ryken *et al.* (Downers Grove, Illinois/Leicester: InterVarsity Press, 1998), 308-309.

Black, Hugh. *Friendship* (New York/Chicago/Toronto: Fleming H. Revel Co., 1900).

Stauffer, Richard. *The Humanness of John Calvin* [trans. George H. Shriver (Nashville: Abingdon Press, 1971): Chapter 2, 'Friend', 47-71].

Stevens, R. Paul. 'Friendship' in Robert Banks and R. Paul Stevens, eds., *The Complete Book of Everyday Christianity* (Downers Grove, Illinois: InterVarsity Press, 1997), 435-442.

MISSION

Bacukham, Richard. *Bible and Mission. Christian Witness in a Postmodern World* (Carlisle, Cumbria: Paternoster Press/Grand Rapids: Baker Book House, 2003).

Jewett, Robert. 'Paul, Phoebe, and the Spanish Mission' in

Jacob Neusner, ed., *The Social World of Formative Christianity and Judaism* (Philadelphia: Fortress Press, 1988), 142-161.

Masters, Peter. 'The Battle for Souls', *Sword & Trowel* (2005, no.2), 7-15.

O'Brien, Peter. 'The Great Commission of Matthew 28:18-20. A Missionary Mandate or Not?', *The Reformed Theological Review*, 35 (1976), 66-78.

O'Brien, P. T. *Gospel and Mission in the Writings of Paul. An Exegetical and Theological Analysis* (Grand Rapids: Baker Academic, 1995).

Rooy, Sidney H. *The Theology of Missions in the Puritan Tradition. A Study of Representative Puritans: Richard Sibbes, Richard Baxter, John Eliot, Cotton Mather, and Jonathan Edwards* (Grand Rapids: William B. Eerdmans Publ. Co., 1965).

INDEX

A wide range of excellent books on spiritual subjects is available from Evangelical Press. Please write to us for your free catalogue or contact us by e-mail.

Evangelical Press
Faverdale North, Darlington, DL3 0PH England
Evangelical Press USA
P. O. Box 825, Webster, NY 14580 USA

email: sales@evangelicalpress.org

www.evangelicalpress.org